# Job-Hunting Online

5TH EDITION

# JOB-HUNTING ONLINE

## A GUIDE TO

Job Listings * Message Boards

Research Sites * the UnderWeb

Counseling * Networking

Self-Assessment Tools * Niche Sites

MARK EMERY BOLLES & RICHARD NELSON BOLLES

TEN SPEED PRESS
Berkeley | Toronto

Ten Speed Press
PO Box 7123
Berkeley, California 94707
www.tenspeed.com

Distributed in Australia by Simon and Schuster Australia, in Canada by Ten Speed Press Canada, in New Zealand by Southern Publishers Group, in South Africa by Real Books, and in the United Kingdom and Europe by Publishers Group UK.

Cover and text design by Betsy Stromberg

Library of Congress Cataloging-in-Publication Data

Bolles, Mark Emery, 1955–
Job-hunting online / by Mark Emery Bolles & Richard Nelson Bolles. — 5th ed.
p. cm.
Rev. ed. of: Job-hunting on the Internet / Richard Nelson Bolles and Mark Emery Bolles. 4th. ed.
Summary: "Helps job searchers integrate the Internet into an efficient job-hunting strategy"—Provided by publisher.
Includes index.
ISBN 978-1-58008-899-2
1. Job hunting—United States—Computer network resources. 2. Web sites—United States—Directories. I. Bolles, Richard Nelson. II. Bolles, Richard Nelson. Job-hunting on the Internet. III. Title.
HF5382.75.U6B65 2008
025.06'65014—dc22

2007046725

Printed in the United States of America

3 4 5 6 7 8 9 10 — 12 11 10 09

# CONTENTS

# INTRODUCTION

**When this book was** first published, the Internet was still pretty much in its infancy, the domain of academics and computer professionals. The idea of the average person using it for job-hunting was fairly revolutionary.

Now here we are, not very many years later, and in that short time the Internet has become an integral part of our society. We use it to email friends and relatives, read the latest news, get the weather report, check on traffic, go shopping, download music, catch TV episodes we might have missed, research questions on practically any subject—the list is endless.

And in the same way, the Internet has become an integral part of the job-hunting process. Any job-hunters who fail to access the information, contacts, job listings, and research opportunities that the Internet has to offer are putting themselves at a serious disadvantage.

As the Internet has changed, so have the techniques and methods of internet job-hunting; so it is natural that this book would change over the years as well. This fifth edition represents a complete rewrite and reorganization of past material, along with much new information and advice to help you find the job you want. This book—along with the most recent edition of *What Color Is Your Parachute?*—provides the most up-to-date information and techniques available for job-hunting in the internet age.

Well, that's all fine to say—but you are probably wondering, Just what, specifically, will I learn from this book that will help me in my job hunt? It's a fair question and one best answered by looking at what the Internet has to offer when you are looking for employment.

## ADVICE

Part of what has made the Internet so popular is its sense of equality. Before the Internet, the economics of publishing made it at least likely that what you were reading—book, newspaper, magazine—came from people who knew what they were talking about. But on the Internet, just about anyone can write, post, and upload whatever they feel like, regardless of whether it's a subject they know anything about. The voice of authority is missing from many websites, and there is far more bad advice than good all over the Internet.

And naturally, there is a *huge* amount of advice on the Internet about job-hunting. There are special sites that exist solely to teach you how to conduct your job hunt effectively. Some are better than others—in fact, some are excellent and some are just awful. How are you to know the difference?

When you are job-hunting, time is your enemy. You cannot afford to waste time on bad advice—and on a subject this important, you desperately need good advice. This book will direct you to the job-hunting advice and information sites that are good and will help you steer clear of the ones that are not. For example, there are websites that I refer to as *Gateways*, which will act as portals for you during your job hunt. By starting at these gateway sites, you will have access to information, articles, and links that will aid you greatly during your job hunt.

## RESUMES

Just as job-hunters go to the Internet looking for job listings, employers go to the Internet looking for resumes. It would be nice if they were actually looking for skilled people—and if you were to ask them, that's what they would claim to be looking for—but really, they are looking for the right resume, rather than the right person. It's not the employer's fault. He believes that one is the same as the other; but of course they are not.

Left to their own devices, most people will not only fail to write a good resume, they will also tend to use their resume badly. If used properly, your resume makes your odds of getting hired much better. But used badly, even a good resume can leave you in the unemployment line. This book, and the websites I point you to, will help you understand what makes a good resume, what makes a bad one, and how you should and should not use this most important instrument.

## JOB LISTINGS

When you think of using the Internet for job-hunting, the first thing you probably think of is job listings—doesn't the Internet have a whole bunch of job listings? You know, Monster, CareerBuilder—those places? And the answer is yes, of course it does; there are millions of job listings on the Internet. But then another question may come to mind: if there are so many job listings, easily found by anyone who watches Super Bowl commercials, why are there all of these books about internet job-hunting? Why doesn't everyone with a computer have a job?

Surveys have shown that when using job listings alone, the success rate for internet job-hunting is pretty dismal: between 4 percent and 10 percent. But there are ways to improve these odds; this book directs you to the websites, search tools, and job-hunting techniques that work, and steers you away from those that don't.

## NETWORKING

The first thing an employer does when he has an opening is to ask the people he knows—friends, present employees, fellow employers—whether they know of anyone available. The first thing a job-hunter does is ask the people he knows—friends, relatives, fellow employees, former fellow employees—if they know of any jobs. In modern parlance, we call this *networking*, and job-hunting studies consistently show that networking has a higher success rate than almost any other single job-hunting method.

The Internet's ability to bridge distance—both geographical and social—makes it a natural tool for networking and developing contacts. Some of the most successful websites are devoted solely to networking and social interaction, and there are chat rooms and forums for every field and subject imaginable. Knowing how to find these and use them in your job hunt can be critical to success.

## COUNSELING AND TESTING

Many job-hunters are in the midst of a career change—or wish they were. But they are often a bit lost and ask themselves, What can I do? What am I good at? What job titles do my skills translate to? To answer these questions, there are places on the Internet designed to help you discern what your best skills are and which ones you most enjoy using (these days, the popular phrase is "motivated skills"), along with methods of turning skill lists into fields and job titles.

And if you are stuck in your job hunt, unsure of where to turn next, there are places where you can get one-on-one counseling with professionals. This book even shows you where such counseling is offered for free.

## RESEARCH

I'll say it again: the Internet is all about information; and boy, there's a lot of it. So much that we have to use special tools (*search engines*) to wade through it all and find what we are looking for. There is so much information out there, in fact, that we are often surprised when the Internet *doesn't* have the information we want . . . but it's actually more likely that we didn't know how to ask the question correctly.

Research is critical to a successful job hunt, particularly if you are entering a new field, changing careers, or moving to a new community. Internet research skills are not only useful during the job hunt, but they are also highly prized by employers and necessary in many jobs. A large part of this book is dedicated to finding information on the Internet.

The organization of this book follows this list exactly. Chapter by chapter, you'll learn how the Internet can best be used to help you land the job you want. Moreover, this book is part of Ten Speed Press's *Parachute* job-hunting series, which is centered around *What Color Is Your Parachute?*—the best-selling job-hunting book of all time, with more than nine million copies in print and rising. *Parachute*'s popularity is easy to understand: the ideas expressed in the book have been well tested over more than three decades and have helped *millions* of people find work—and not just any work, but work that they love to do. Your job hunt will be most successful, online and off, if you have a strategy that follows the three central themes of *Parachute*, which can be summed up as WHAT, WHERE, and HOW:

- Discover *what* your best and most enjoyable skills are.
- Choose *where* you want to use these skills by identifying the fields of interest, geographical area, and the working conditions in which you will use them.
- Decide *how* you will go about finding this job by identifying the organizations that interest you most and finding the person there with the power to hire.

Used well, the Internet can serve as an integral part of your job-hunting strategy and will greatly increase your chances of achieving job-hunting success. As an important volume in the *Parachute* series, this book shows you how to use the Internet to get you to work as quickly as possible, doing the kind of work you most enjoy.

## WHEN LESS IS MORE

Though largely forgotten these days, the dot-com crash of some years ago taught us two important lessons. The first is, *Don't give your life savings to a bunch of twenty-three year olds.* (Amazing so many people never thought of this.) The second is, *People don't want a hundred choices for everything*. How many grocery stores do you shop at? How many dry cleaners do you go to? How many different routes do you take on your way to work? People want to have a reasonable number of options to choose from, but they don't want to be overwhelmed. Studies have borne this out: if you see a table at the grocery store selling four different kinds of jam, sales double; if they offer forty kinds, sales tumble to almost nothing.

We can apply the same principle to books about the Internet. You may have noticed that many books about the Internet are nothing but a long list of website addresses, essentially leaving to you the work of figuring out which ones will work best. With an estimated forty thousand job-related sites on the Internet, listing even 10 percent of these would be useless to you. You don't want to know every job site available; you want to know which ones will be most helpful to you in your job hunt.

So, rather than being a complete index of internet job-hunting sites, this book is a collection of carefully chosen ones, sites that I think will help you find the work you want, quickly and efficiently. If I didn't think that a site would be helpful, or if there were many others better in its category, then that site was not listed in the book. Only the best (in my opinion) made it in.

And, from among those chosen few, I have further narrowed the field by selecting those that I think are *especially* good, and I have called them Parachute Picks, with a Parachute symbol alongside their listing, thus:

This means that for job-hunting purposes, this is one of the best sites on the Internet, in the category it is listed in.

With the sites that I *have* listed, I have tried to be honest about what they have to offer and what they don't. In some cases, I will recommend a site for doing *this* thing but not for doing *that*. You need to know the difference if you're going to find the work that you want to do as quickly as possible, using the Internet.

## INTERNET ACCESS

Naturally, to use this book effectively, you will need a computer with Internet access. If you don't have one, at home or at work (or have a friend who will let you use theirs), you can usually find one that you can rent for a fee, or sometimes use for free, by going to any of the following:

- A commercial establishment that offers free or low-fee wireless Internet access. Coffee shops, cafes, bookstores, print shops—the list is constantly growing.
- Your local public library.
- Your local state or government employment center.
- Internet kiosks in all kinds of public places, including airports, stadiums, hotels, cruise ships, and freeway rest stops.

As soon as you line up one online session, you can identify more options. Check the list of thousands of establishments offering Internet access at *The Cybercafe Search Engine* web page at **http://cybercaptive.com/pia.shtml**. A similar list of some 4,200 Internet cafes in 141 countries can be found at **www.cybercafes.com**. Also try these sites:

**www.hotspot-locations.com**
**www.wi-fihotspotlist.com**
**http://wi-fi.jiwire.com**
**www.wififreespot.com**

## FOR-FEE SITES $$

The Internet's popularity is due, in great part, to the fact that it is essentially free. Most attempts to turn the Internet into a fee-for-service business—at least in the job-hunting world—have (I am happy to say) met with failure, and you will find that most websites do not charge for access. But there are exceptions, occasionally even worthy ones, and as you go about your job hunt on the Internet, you will find some sites that are fee-driven, generally involving subscriptions allowing access to specific data for a certain length of time. As always when on the Internet, be careful when reaching for your credit card: security is no small issue.

And as for whether you should spend money at all, don't let desperation in your job hunt make "buy/don't buy" decisions for you. I have identified fee-for-service sites in this book with dollar signs, thus: $$

Note that many of these fee-for-service sites will allow you free access for a certain trial period.

## USING THIS BOOK

Throughout this book, I have listed the URLs, or addresses, of the various websites under discussion. Not only is it a pain to type all of these URLs into a web browser, but it is easy to make mistakes. To solve this problem, you may go to the *Job-Hunter's Bible* website at

**www.jobhuntersbible.com**

where you will find a regularly updated collection of all of the hyperlinks in this book. You can click on them from the site or import the links into your Favorites or Bookmarks for easy use. This will bring you to the site you want with a single click, avoiding the laborious typing of URLs.

A note on grammar: although this book is a collaborative endeavor, to maintain a conversational tone we have elected to use the pronoun "I" instead of "we."

## BOOK UPDATES

Writing a book about the Internet is like taking a snapshot of the weather: initially accurate but unlikely to be so for long. The Internet is constantly changing; links are broken, pages move, and web addresses can become obsolete. If you find a URL that doesn't work, either in this book or at the *Job-Hunter's Bible* website, please let me know immediately, at **jobhunter@wt.net**.

In spite of spending more time than I want to think about on the Internet, I'm certain there are a lot of good sites about which I know nothing—at least, not yet. If you, as a job-hunter, find a site that was particularly useful to you in your job hunt, and you therefore think it should be listed in the next edition of this book, please let me know, again by sending an email to **jobhunter@wt.net**. And if you operate a site that you think would be helpful to other readers (and it isn't a resume distribution service or other scheme that you know runs counter to the central ideas in *Parachute*), please let me know, at the same address.

# 1. GETTING STARTED

**Back in 1985,** the late John Crystal used to describe the ridiculousness of our traditional job-hunting "system." A job-hunter, he said, would be walking down a street, despairing of ever finding the work he or she wanted, and brushing past him, with a hurried "Excuse me," would be an employer who was hunting desperately for exactly that man or woman with exactly those talents and experience. But that would be the last they would ever see of each other. Our job-hunting "system" had not yet come up with any good way for them to find each other, so instead, they would pass like ships in the night.

So the act—or maybe it would be better to call it the *art*—of job-hunting is the process of making sure that, rather than passing each other, these two people will bump into each other and start a conversation. There are a number of ways to do this, and time has shown that each has an average success rate. Here are the most common job-hunting methods and their rates of success:

1. Put your resume on an internet career site, like Monster or CareerBuilder. The odds that you will find a job this way average out to about 4 percent. Or stated another way, for every hundred people that try this, ninety-six will remain unemployed. (Well . . . if you're in the IT field, your chances rise to about 10 percent, so only ninety people will remain jobless. Best to be optimistic.)

2. Send out resumes to employers at random. Success rate: 7 percent.

3. Answer newspaper ads. The success rate varies a bit; at the lower salary levels, such as the trades and labor-intensive jobs,

the success rate can be as high as 24 percent. For higher salary levels, success is around 5 percent.

4. Go to your local unemployment office: 14 percent.

5. Go to a private employment agency: 5 percent. (This figure refers to placement firms, not the traditional temporary services like Manpower and Kelly Girl.)

6. Ask everyone you can think of if they know of a job opening. The success rate rises to 33 percent or better.

7. Go knocking on doors of any place you can think of, whether they are known to have an opening or not: average success rate is 47 percent. This is more likely to work for, say, secretaries than for corporate CEOs. If you want to be the head of General Motors, there might be better ways. The online version of this—scattering emails and resumes randomly around the Internet—is spectacularly unsuccessful these days, as such uninvited submissions are typically considered spam and dealt with accordingly.

8. Identify the firms in your area doing the kind of work you are good at and contact them to see if they need someone like you. The success rate is about 69 percent.

9. Do the kind of creative job hunt outlined in this book and described in great detail in *What Color Is Your Parachute?* This method has a success rate of 86 percent.

When you look at these methods and success rates, there are a few things you should note:

- The less successful methods are the ones that are essentially passive in nature. If you wait around, hoping the right job falls into your lap, you are more likely to remain unemployed. On the other hand, the more you take the active role and go out and work at your job hunt, the more successful you will be.

- The less successful methods start out with, and rely heavily on, a resume. The more successful methods do not. I'll explore this in more depth later in the book, but for now, think about it: employers don't want to hire a resume; they want to hire a person. But not all job-hunters know how to translate themselves into a resume, and not all employers know how to read a resume and see the person behind it. In most cases, you should do everything you can to *not* show your prospective employer a resume, unless and until you absolutely have to.

- The success rates I have given you are for when someone tries *only* that single method. When you use more than one method, the success rates become cumulative. So don't rely on any one method of job-hunting. Use more than one. Just remember that, strangely enough, when people try to use more than three methods, the success rates start going down.

- Last, try to think of the preceding statistics in a new way. Rather than looking at them as success or failure rates—hard limits, about which you can do little—think of them as a gauge to how much time you should put into using each of those methods during your job hunt; this is far more empowering. So, for example, go ahead and put your resume up on Monster and check out the positions that are posted at various websites—but don't spend more than 10 percent of your job-hunting time doing it. Similarly, don't spend more than 5 percent of your job-hunting time answering want ads.

And if all of these statistics still depress you, just remember the old joke that says that 86 percent of all statistics are made up on the spot.

Of the nine job-hunting methods I have listed, the first eight are variations on what we might call the traditional job hunt. This is essentially a matching game: you compare a list of skills you have against a list of skills an employer needs, and if the two match closely enough, you apply for the position. If the prospective employer agrees that you are a close match to what they want, then you'll be hired. Often, there may be no actual list of skills—you may summarize the skills under a job title, like "carpenter" or "systems analyst"—but it's still the same thing: you have a certain view of what you can do and are looking for a pigeonhole into which you can fit yourself, for the sake of employment.

The ninth method—the *Parachute*-style, creative job hunt—is more complex and takes more work, but it will usually reward you with more job satisfaction, a higher salary, and greater personal fulfillment.

Much of this extra work is devoted to research about yourself and about prospective work places. To accomplish it properly, this type of job hunt requires you to do three things:

1. Carefully inventory your skills, particularly the ones you most enjoy using, so that you know what it is you want to be doing with half of your waking life.
2. Define in what field of endeavor, and under what conditions, you want to use these skills.
3. Research those organizations you want to work for, who are in need of the skills you possess. (At times, you may find that an organization that interests you may not have an actual job opening, but if you identify the person in that organization with the power to hire, and demonstrate to that person that you have the skills to solve their problems, then they will often create a position for you.)

The job hunt that you need to perform right now may be somewhere in between the traditional and the creative approaches. No single method is always 100-percent successful; some methods work better for certain people than for others. As a job-hunter, you must assess your current situation, make some decisions on how you will go about your job hunt, and come up with a strategy—a plan for how you are going to approach this challenge in your life.

It is beyond the scope of this book to teach you such strategies in sufficient detail. For that, you should pick up a recent copy of *What Color Is Your Parachute?* (I say "recent," because it is updated every year, as the world changes) and read it cover to cover. When you have done that, then this book will be far more effective in showing you how to use the tremendous resources of the Internet during your job hunt.

Unfortunately, most people have a skewed impression of what the Internet can do for them when they go job-hunting. Websites like Monster and CareerBuilder have given the impression that all you have to do is put your resume on their site, and within a day or two—if it even takes *that* long—firm job offers will arrive in your email. In the real world, this happens only rarely; but even the possibility of finding a job with such ease can be quite seductive. The real shame of it, though, is that it causes people to view the Internet as a *solution* to job-hunting rather than just one part of their *approach* to job-hunting.

If you can learn to see going online as just one of the resources you are using in your job-hunt—and learn how to use that resource well, along with your other resources—then you will be that much closer to finding the meaningful work you seek. Throughout this book, I'll examine the most common job-hunting methods just listed and look at what the Internet has to offer for each of them.

## PARTS OF THE INTERNET

Before we dive too deeply into how to approach the Internet when we are job-hunting, we should look at what the Internet is. The Internet has different parts; four of them are useful in your job hunt.

### The World Wide Web

Originally, the Internet was just a network that allowed the military—and later, universities and other learning institutions—to link their computers together. Certain rules and standards were established to define how the computers would all talk to each other; these were called *protocols*. (Before computers, this word was most often associated with matters of diplomacy, referring to conduct and etiquette used when people communicated with each other. It's easy to see the parallels.)

Though many of the older protocols are still in use, the Internet did not achieve its amazing popularity until the invention of *hypertext* and HyperText Transport Protocol, or HTTP. It is hypertext, HTTP, and the language used to implement hypertext pages (HyperText Markup Language, or HTML) that has made the World Wide Web possible. The Web is now so dominant that when most people say "Internet," it is the Web that they are referring to. But you should remember that the Web is just one part of the Internet, though it is the largest part and the one most responsible for the Internet's commercial success and its penetration into our everyday lives.

Practically speaking—protocols and alphabet soup aside—the Web consists of the hyperlinked pages that you view with a browser program, such as Internet Explorer, Firefox, or Safari. By clicking on a link in the page you are currently viewing, you can be instantly transported to another page, which may be on a computer next door or on the other side of the planet. The process is transparent, the serving computer's actual location trivial. When speaking of "websites," "sites," "pages," and so on, we are, with rare exceptions, referring to the World Wide Web. And it is on the Web that job-hunters will find most of the information relevant to their search for employment.

When people are first introduced to the Web, they are usually told to think of the Web as an almost infinite series of library rooms, each with many doors. As you enter through one door, you may find yourself in a room filled with information. The information can take a variety of forms; usually it is written, but it could also be in the form of pictures, audio recordings, videos, and so on, though these are generally not as helpful to the job-hunter.

In any room, some of the data may be useful, some not. You can read what is in this particular room, or you may choose to click on a link that will take you through one of the available doorways to find yourself in other rooms, each with more data and more doorways. Maybe the information in the new room is more useful to you than in the last; maybe you will have to go through many rooms before you find what you want. In each room, you may stay and read or go back to one of the rooms you were already in, where there were other doors, to other library rooms, each with interesting possibilities for you to try. Some of the rooms are small; some are huge. Some rooms are filled with fascinating books; others are useless. Some contain information that can be wrong, even offensive. Some rooms exist solely to serve as gateways to other rooms. Ultimately, all of the rooms, all over the World Wide Web, are interconnected with each other; hence the name.

Many rooms on the Web exist specifically for job-hunting. There are websites dedicated to helping job-hunters and employers find each other. Others teach people the techniques of job-hunting (using the Internet and otherwise). There are sites dedicated to helping people find other people with common interests, geographies, education, fields of employment, and so on. There are sites useful for researching companies, fields, people, and places, as well as anything else pertaining to what you want to do, where you want to do it, and how you might go about it. And if you are feeling a bit fuzzy on any of these matters, there are sites that offer counseling, testing, and advice for the job-hunter.

Many other websites may not exist specifically for the job-hunter but are still useful in your search. Sometimes such sites are obvious: for example, most companies have a website where you can find financial data, company size, contact information, and so on. Sometimes the information may be more subtle: What other businesses are in the same area as the company you are researching? Is the local economy growing? What are crime rates like where you are considering working? What is the cost of living like in that area? What is the government's take on the future of the fields you are looking at? Any place you can find out information regarding yourself—your skills, the fields that interest you, where you might be working, who there has the power to hire you, and so on—is grist for your job-hunting mill. Most of this is available online.

## Email

Daily email access is essential for your job hunt. It has become a standard form of business communication, and you will also find that your email address serves as a common method of identifying yourself. Many websites that you will visit during your job hunt demand some form of registration for complete access. These websites will usually require your email address for the registration process, and many use your email address to identify you. If you want to post your resume at any of the job sites online, it is through email that prospective employers will contact you. When you set up an interview for a job, notification will likely be through email.

And of course, email is not limited to your computer; PDAs and many cell phones have email capabilities. As email gains this kind of portability, its use will become even more common and access to it more necessary. (By 2010, Nokia expects four billion people to have cell service with some sort of web connectivity.) The day may not be far off when your street address is less important than your email address.

## Usenet

Although its use has declined greatly, there is a part of the Internet known as Usenet that may, in some cases, be useful to you in your job hunt. Usenet is a contraction of *User Network*. (In fact, just to be technical, Usenet is not a part of the Internet, but it is accessible *through* the Internet.) Usenet allows you to view what are called *newsgroups*; these are generally communication threads, similar to web forums. You can access all of the newsgroups your ISP allows by using a newsreader client program such as Free Agent or Xnews. You can also access many newsgroups by using your web browser to view Google's newsgroup index, though Google's index is not complete in every area.

Newsgroups are like chat rooms, where people with similar interests can post articles, comments, gripes, pictures, and, occasionally, even news. As of this writing, the number of newsgroups exceeds one hundred thousand. Let's say that again: there are over *one hundred thousand* different newsgroups, most of them on different subjects. As I write, about twenty thousand are currently active.

Some of the subjects are quite general, such as people who are interested in photography. Others are more narrow in scope, such as people who are interested in black-and-white photography of mountains in Southern Chile or who listen to East Coast thrash metal music. We begin to understand why there are so many—and why not all remain active.

An unfortunately large number of newsgroups are devoted to the less noble aspects of human nature. But some are, if not devoted to job-hunting, at least useful for certain aspects of some job hunts. Regardless of your occupation or field of interest, there is undoubtedly a newsgroup devoted to it where you can find others with the same interests as you. There you may make the contacts or find the information that will help you land your next job. For the most part, you will find that technical and academic fields are more likely to make use of newsgroups and Usenet than other fields.

Usenet's drawbacks are obvious. There are so many newsgroups that finding the ones that will help you in your job hunt can be difficult. And, to be honest, there is a lot of dreck posted in newsgroups. If nothing else, the Internet has given everyone with a computer and a phone line complete equality to say whatever they want (and as much) to the whole wired world.

### Listserv

Commonly referred to as *mailing lists*, these are discussion groups that take place using email. Unlike most email, which is most often direct communication between two people, mailing lists are discussions sent to everyone who happens to be a member of that list. These discussions are archived and searchable. Sometimes, jobs and resumes are distributed this way as well.

Many subjects are covered—there are roughly four hundred thousand different mailing lists—though not all are public. There are websites where you will find directories of available mailing lists.

## COMMON SENSE AND THE INTERNET

Some readers of this book will be newcomers to the Internet, forced into an area they had, until now, resisted entering. This is not a primer on how to use your computer or the Internet, so for those of you who are new to all of this, try visiting the following websites. They provide tips on using the Internet safely and securely.

### Learn the Net: The Internet Owner's Manual

**www.learnthenet.com/english/index.html**

A really delightful site—fun and interesting. If you know nothing about the Internet, how it works, or how to use it, this is the first place to go. And even if you already know a lot, it's still helpful. An unusual quality.

### Basic Web Lessons

**www.aarp.org/learntech/computers/basic_web/**

An excellent tutorial from the good folks at AARP.

### Internet Tips: Protect Your PC and Data with the Security Checklist

**www.pcworld.com/article/id,109377-page,1/article.html**

A good article from the people who know on safeguarding your computer and information.

### Computer Security Primer—The Internet

**http://guide2net.net/tcpip/columns/security_internet/**

A basic primer on security issues when using the Internet.

### Protect Yourself: Security Tips

**www.learnthenet.com/english/html/79secure.htm**

A short and sweet article on internet security.

In addition to the information at these sites, let me give you a few basic cautions. Though it has brought great benefits, the wide reach of the Internet has brought risks as well. Other than criminal scams and security threats (spyware, malware, adware, and the like), the primary risks when job-hunting are data smog and bad information.

*Data smog* is that sense of being overwhelmed by the unbelievable wealth of information available online. If you have even a slightly curious mind, you can easily be led astray by your own interest in the world around you. When you go online, make sure that you have a specific idea of what you are looking for. Plan your research; try not to surf. You can waste many hours, all the while telling yourself how hard you are working on your job hunt.

That brings us to bad information.

A few years ago, the city councilors in Alisa Viejo, California, scheduled a vote on whether to ban Styrofoam cups at city events, because they learned that Styrofoam manufacture involves the use of dihydrogen monoxide, or DHMO. Much of their information on DHMO came from a website dedicated to educating the public about the dangers of this chemical, located at **www.dhmo.org/facts.html**.

And the information is frightening indeed. Consider:

- As stated on the website, "DHMO is a constituent of many known toxic substances, diseases and disease-causing agents, environmental hazards and can even be lethal to humans in quantities as small as a thimbleful."
- Inhaling even a small amount of DHMO can cause death.
- The gaseous form of DHMO can cause severe burns on human skin.
- Prolonged exposure to the solid form of DHMO causes severe tissue damage.
- DHMO is a major component of acid rain.
- Research conducted by award-winning U.S. scientist Nathan Zohner concluded that roughly 86 percent of the population supports a ban on dihydrogen monoxide.

No wonder the Alisa Viejo city council wanted to remove all associations with this dangerous chemical.

The problem is that the term *dihydrogen monoxide* is another way of saying $H_2O$, or water. And it is all true: water is a major component of acid rain; breathing even small amounts will kill you, though we usually call it *drowning*; the gaseous form, known as *steam*, can cause burns; and prolonged direct exposure to the solid form (ice) causes tissue damage, known as *frostbite*. As for Nathan Zohner, he *is* an award-winning scientist. He won a prize in a science fair when he was fourteen years old (he's probably in college by now). When he told people about the dangers of DHMO and asked fifty people if they thought it should be banned, forty-three of them said yes.

Although this is a fun example to bring up, I have a point here. We are used to trusting what we read. The economic realities of book, newspaper, and magazine publishing (with some help from Western culture's litigious nature) have helped to ensure that most published information is generally trustworthy. When the trust is broken—as with Jayson Blair, Jack Kelley, and Stephen Glass—it is major news itself.

But now we have the Internet. And even more than the printing press, the Internet is the great equalizer; you can create and maintain a website for less money than most teenagers spend on CDs. That means that the truth bar could be high, or it could be dropped on the floor with a loud *clang*. And there usually is no one, other than yourself, who can tell you where the bar is at any given moment.

Obviously, the DHMO website is a satire; it is not meant to intentionally mislead. And the vast majority of things you will read on the Internet are at least *believed* to be true by the people who write and publish them—but that doesn't mean the information is always accurate. So when you are on the Internet, use some care: try to confirm your data with multiple sources; consider the provenance of the content, who wrote it and why. When using internet-based information for your job hunt, take extra care to make sure it is correct.

## DEALING WITH CHANGING WEB ADDRESSES

The addresses of web pages are constantly changing; it is the nature of the Internet. The reasons are many, and ultimately, not important; it's just one of those things we have to accept, like traffic jams and beer commercials. As you use this book, it is inevitable that you will find some "bad" web addresses: you type in (or click on) the URL for a site and get some kind of page error. This means that between the time this book was published and the time you got to a certain web page, something changed. What do you do?

Nine times out of ten, the page is still there . . . somewhere. You just need to find it. Here are a few techniques you can try.

First, go to Google (or whatever search engine you prefer) and, as the search query, type the name of the entry I have given you. Let's use this example:

The Dirty Dozen Online Job Search Mistakes

**www.job-hunt.org/jobsearchmistakes.shtml**

For this example, your search term is "dirty dozen online job search mistakes," although you can also try shorter versions like "dozen job search mistakes" or "dozen job mistakes."

When the search engine comes back with its search return page, look at the entries; are any of them at the correct website (**www.job-hunt.org**)? If so, click on that entry, and the correct page will probably come up.

If none of the entries match, or you still get a page error, then try this: enter the entry's title, just like last time, but follow it with the *site* command (explained in this book's Online Research section), and the domain of the website. This command varies with different search engines; with Google, it would look like this:

**dozen online job search mistakes site:www.job-hunt.org**

This forces Google to only look on the job-hunt website for your search term. (A domain is the part of the URL after "http://" and up to the first single forward slash. Check out some of the internet tutorials I recommend to learn more about domains; all have good explanations.)

If you still haven't found the right page, the next thing to try is URL chopping. Since URLs are hierarchical in nature, you are trying to make the URL less specific; so you chop off the right-most section of the URL, starting from the slash that is nearest the right hand side. Here is an example:

**www.thejobspider.com/job/directory/employment-resources.asp**

In this case, you would chop off "employment-resources.asp," leaving only **www.thejobspider.com/job/directory/**, and then press the Enter key. If this results in a good page, then look around for a hyperlink or other reference to the page you want; or try using the site's Search function, if one is available.

On the other hand, if you still get a page error, chop off the next right-most section ("directory/"), and so forth. If you get all the way down to just the domain—in this case **www.thejobspider.com**—and you still get an error, a page that makes no sense, or an offer to buy the domain, then chances are that the website has in fact disappeared and not just had a change of address. Go back to step one, where you were Googling the title of the entry, and see if any of the other search returns look helpful to you. Sometimes, a slight rewording of the search term will reveal what was previously hidden; and in rare cases, you may find that the site, or its data, is not to be had. Well, that's the Internet for you, and the reason why most categories in this book have multiple entries.

Lastly, if you keep your eyes open, you will probably notice that the web pages that are most likely to disappear without warning are the ones that end with .asp or .php. This indicates some of the newer programming technologies, which are capable of generating user-specific or time-specific web pages. If you approach the same page from a different direction than the last time you were there, the URL can sometimes change significantly.

Now that we have had a little bit of familiarization with the Internet, let's look at some of the basic advice that's available for the job-hunter.

# JOB-HUNTING: ONLINE GUIDES

There are online job-hunting manuals everywhere on the Web. Their general quality has increased enormously since this book was first published, but the first two still stand out:

## Creative Job Search

**www.deed.state.mn.us/cjs/cjsbook/index.htm**

This site, maintained by Minnesota's Department of Employment and Economic Development, has put together the equivalent of a job-search manual. A superior example of the breed.

## Career Development eManual

**www.cdm.uwaterloo.ca/**

Here is another excellent guide—they call it an eManual—from the Career Center at the University of Waterloo in Ontario, Canada. Its self-assessment section is one of the best on the Internet; naturally, the links throughout the site tend to be Canada-centric.

## CollegeGrad.com Job Search

**www.collegegrad.com/jobsearch/intro.shtml**

Author Brian Krueger's book, *College Grad Job-hunter*, though available in bookstores, is also available online, free, and well translated into web (hyperlinked) format. The book is aimed at the college graduate, emphasizing techniques to use when you have book learning but not much real-world experience. He also points out that job-hunting is an experience that you should start preparing for before it happens, and there is a lot of good advice for all job-hunters. I think that some of his guerrilla tactics should be avoided, but this is a minor complaint; it's a great online resource.

## Job Search Strategies and Resources for Graduate Students

**www.bc.edu/offices/careers/resourcesfor/gradstudents.html**

From Boston College, this is a Powerpoint presentation with some good tips. This one is also aimed at graduates without extensive work experience but still has much of value. Also, check out BC's other career resources at **www.bc.edu/offices/careers/resourcesfor/gradstudents/#professional**.

### Career Playbook

**www.careerplaybook.com/guide/tour_overview.asp**

If you don't mind the football analogy central to this site, this is a pretty good guide. It stresses the importance of having a plan for your job hunt and backs it up with good advice.

## JOB-HUNTING: ONLINE ARTICLES

The Web is brimming with articles about job-hunting. As time passes, it's becoming more difficult to find the ones that burn brightest in a field that always tends to generate more heat than light. The ones I have listed here are all good, for various reasons. There will be more links to articles about internet research, contacts, resumes, and job boards as we get to those chapters.

### The Truth about Online Job-Hunting

**www.careerjournal.com/jobhunting/usingnet/20020417-needleman.html**

Though not extensive or earthshaking, this article is a good, basic primer on internet job-hunting. More about attitudes than actions, the article will help to dispel a number of false assumptions and point you down the right road. You'll find many helpful articles on the *Wall Street Journal* website. Explore it thoroughly.

### Survival Guide to Job-Hunting

**www.infotoday.com/searcher/jul02/mort.htm**

If you read only one article for your job hunt, this should be the one. A sidebar also explains why Monster (and job boards in general) are not the success we might hope they would be.

### Common Job Search Misconceptions

**www.wetfeet.com/asp/article.asp?aid=105&atype=Interviewing**

A very good article, and if you browse the WetFeet site, you'll find many others of the same quality.

### The Dirty Dozen Online Job-Hunting Mistakes

**www.job-hunt.org/jobsearchmistakes.shtml**

Another good one, from one of the best gateway job sites.

### Forum: Ask the Hiring Manager

**www.collegegrad.com/forum/index.shtml**

This particular page is a series of questions answered by author Brian Krueger, about different aspects of the job hunt. On the same site, check out the e-zine at **www.collegegrad.com/ezine/index.shtml**, where you will find a list of links to past articles.

### The Info Pro's Survival Guide to Job-Hunting

**www.infotoday.com/searcher/jul02/mort.htm**

This is a good article by Mary Ellen Mort. Although it's written for librarians and information professionals and thus somewhat advanced for most readers at this stage of the game, Mort makes some interesting points about why traditional techniques offer such poor success rates, and she gives a number of tips on finding the Hidden Job Market.

## GATEWAYS

When beginning your internet job hunt, it is helpful to start where you will find the largest amount of useful information in the least amount of time. I call these sites *Gateways*.

Gateways are starting places, doorways to the Internet, specifically organized for the job-hunter by people who are experts in the field (well, at least for the Gateways I have listed). So rather than typing "job-hunting" into a search engine and then having to deal with the 17.7 million (Google), 24.4 million (Yahoo!), or 91 million (yikes . . . that one is Clusty) entries that are returned, you can instead go to the Gateway sites, secure in the knowledge that people who know what they are doing have already done the searching, sifting, organizing, and evaluating.

The best Gateways are well-organized information clearinghouses. They have articles about various aspects of the job hunt, in which you can learn more about the *process* of job-hunting and how to go about it effectively. They have links to other sites on the Web where you can find even more information relevant to your particular job hunt. Because the links you will find at these Gateways have all been vetted by knowledgeable people, you will save huge amounts of time and energy by going to them first, rather than trying to sift through the avalanche of information that a general search engine would provide.

Here are the best:

## Job-Hunt

**www.job-hunt.org**

Here you will find a wealth of information on job-hunting and using the Internet effectively as well as current articles about the world of work. In addition, there are many links to job-search resources and industry journals, organized by field, location, and so on. This site is extremely well organized; I find that the *look* of a website is crucial to using that site well and finding the information that it has to offer. I really like the look of Job-Hunt.

## JobStar

**www.jobstar.org**

Originally a California site—and still somewhat California-centric—JobStar has a national presence, with lots of good information for the job-hunter. JobStar is particularly good when looking for information on salaries and the Hidden Job Market. (If you don't know what I mean by that, you have obviously *not* read *What Color Is Your Parachute?* and shame on you!) Because the site's funding is from the California State Library, there are links to actual job postings in California, with specific JobStar sites for Los Angeles, San Diego, Sacramento, and San Francisco; this also explains why there are not specific sites for areas outside of California. But JobStar does have links to help you find work, regardless of location, and most of the site's information is relevant, no matter where you live. Definitely one of the best job-hunting sites on the Web.

## Job-Hunter's Bible

**www.jobhuntersbible.com**

This is the companion website for readers of the books in the *What Color Is Your Parachute?* series. Here you will find many articles, links, and resources for the job-hunter. The site is organized very much like this book, and each internet site and URL in this book is available on the site with just a few clicks. For greatest efficiency, make Job-Hunter's Bible your home page during your job search.

## The Riley Guide

**www.rileyguide.com**

An extremely comprehensive site, thanks to its creator, Margaret F. Dikel (formerly Margaret Riley, hence the name). What you get here is a well-organized, manageable index of job-hunting resources on the Internet plus a lot of extras, like a summary of resume databases and job-search guides. In addition to informative (and timely) articles, there are many links to job listings by industry and profession, from "Academic Librarians" to "Zoo and Aquarium." If I was to note any weakness in the site, it would be its completeness (which, of course, is also one of its main strengths). There is a lot of information here, and it may take you a little while to become familiar enough with the site to find exactly what you want. But this is a minor complaint; in balance, the Riley Guide is one of the best places to start your job hunt.

## CareerOneStop

**www.careeronestop.org**

Sponsored by the U.S. Department of Labor, CareerOneStop is part of an interlinked network of job sites. This network was reorganized in 2007, eliminating the database of jobs and resumes known as America's Job Bank. In addition to CareerOneStop, the network includes America's Career InfoNet, with information about employment trends, training, financial aid, state resources, and links to websites with career information; and America's Service Locator, where you can find various job-hunting resources—information on companies, schools, and state employment development departments—near you.

## CareerJournal

**www.careerjournal.com**

The site's subtitle is "The *Wall Street Journal* Executive Career Site," so I won't be divulging secrets if I say that it is perhaps more excellent for people with MBAs than for those on a blue-collar career path. Be that as it may, there are a lot of resources to be found on the site, including job-hunting advice, salary research, columnists, discussion groups, and so on. Note also that Career Journal is just one of the *WSJ*'s network of internet sites; also of interest to the job-hunter is RealEstateJournal, for when you are moving; StartupJournal, for the self-employed; and CollegeJournal, for those in school and soon to join the work force.

### CollegeGrad.com

**www.collegegrad.com**

This is self-billed as "the #1 entry-level job site." Believe it. Among its features is a large database of employers who are looking for grads and entry-level personnel, and the forum *Ask the Hiring Manager*, in which author Brian Krueger responds to questions posed by job-hunters.

Part of the secret to the site's excellence is that the people here see their mission as a limited one: helping to find employment for college students and recent graduates only. But many of the site's resources are useful to all, and you should have the site in your Favorites (Bookmarks) folder for sure.

### Quintessential Careers

**www.quintcareers.com**
**www.quintcareers.com/portal.html**

There is a lot of stuff here—more than two thousand pages, much of it quite good. Besides all of the stuff you would expect on a gateway site—like articles on job-hunting, resumes, testing, and career assessment—you'll find data on making a career change, the top companies to work for (grouped in categories such as private companies, public companies, multicultural companies, companies that are best for the older worker, and so on), links to resources for teens, for the working college student—*lots* of stuff. Also, the site has many links to colleges and other education resources. The interface is good, the pages are well set up, and the site is logical and, for the most part, easy to use.

Not that the site is perfect—many of the articles lack depth, and not all parts of the site work equally well with all browsers. Still a very useful site for all that.

## THE SUPERSITES

The Supersites are the ones that just about everyone thinks of when you mention internet job-hunting: Monster, CareerBuilder, Yahoo! HotJobs, and so on. These sites are hugely popular. Back in June 2004, in that one month alone, 9.6 million job-seekers were online with Monster; CareerBuilder was right behind, with

9.3 million. A recent survey showed that of all people who were job-hunting online, 89 percent had registered with Monster. Similar figures exist for the other two Supersites.

To understand the Supersites, you have to know a little about how all internet job sites work in general. There are many thousands of sites that accept resumes and job listings. You can think of these job sites as a computer program that matches words in resumes with words in job listings: a "matching engine," if you will. If you work with computers much, you'll recognize that these job sites are just specialized databases with a search function: from an employer's point of view, a database of resumes; for the job-hunter, a database of job listings. It doesn't matter much which direction the task is approached from. However you wish to think of it—matching engine, searchable database—it is wrapped in a (hopefully) attractive package, with articles and other services to assist the job-hunter, and presented on the Web.

The different job sites are pretty much all there to make money; they do this mostly by charging employers to post job listings. (Rarely, the job-hunter may pay a fee, but that is quite unusual.) The different job sites use two basic approaches to convince employers to post listings on their site: one is specialization; the other, size.

Employers are no different from anyone else: they want to get the most for their money. So when they decide to post their job listings on a website, and then wonder which site they should use, they want to go where they believe most job-hunters will go—or at least the kind of job-hunters they want to hire. So if employers are in a niche field—engineering, law enforcement, or health care, for example—they tend to go to a job board that specializes in that field. There are thousands of these specialized job sites on the Internet.

But to many people, the most logical approach is to go for size. Imagine for a moment if there were only one job site on the Internet where people could go to post resumes and job listings. All job openings would be listed there, and all job hunters would place their resumes there as well. Finding a job (or, from the employer's point of view, finding an employee) would be no more difficult than going to this one site.

Of course, this is not the case; but there are sites out there that would sure like you to think it is. These are the Supersites: they count primarily on their size to convince employers that this is where they should post their job listings, because (they claim) *every* job-hunter goes there. And once they have the job listings, then they can say to the job-hunter, hey, we've got more job listings than anyone else, so come to our site—which convinces the employers to post more, which brings more job-hunters, and on it goes, with both sides feeding each other. If you convince enough employers to post their job listings, then you can even afford to buy commercial time during the Super Bowl (which both Monster and CareerBuilder have done).

So the Supersites' financial model depends on their popularity. All well and good, so why is it that out of all the people who go looking for jobs there, only about 4 percent to 10 percent succeed? There are a number of reasons.

One is that not all of the job listings are real jobs. Historically, Monster and CareerBuilder have accepted job listings from agencies, recruiters, and companies that are looking to sell their wares and services to job-hunters but whose listings don't represent real jobs; rather, they are a way of gathering names and addresses. Also, many companies like to keep their "brand" out there for people to see, even when they are not actively hiring at the moment. It's not the Supersites' fault; they can't afford to make sure there is a real job behind every job listing they get, and of course there is the financial pressure to sell more and more job listings.

Another reason that the Supersites don't always work is that the job listings tend to represent jobs that are more difficult to fill. Employers—like job-hunters—like to take the shortest route between two points, as well as the least expensive. When they have a position that needs filling, they first try to hire from within; then they ask their current employees if they know of anyone suitable; then they go to their contacts (their "network"); and it is only when these other methods all fail that they will decide to spend money on filling a vacancy. Posting a job opening with one of the Supersites costs the employer money. So, statistically speaking, the job postings that are on the Supersites tend to be openings that are just a little harder to fill than otherwise, from the employer's point of view, because they would happily fill them without spending the money if they could. From the job-hunter's point of view, this means that the jobs that many Supersite postings represent can be slightly less desirable or require higher levels of experience and education.

Historically, the Supersites have worked better for those in the information technology field and slightly better as well for those with executive, managerial, and technical backgrounds. They have not been very effective at all for low-tech and manufacturing jobs and what we traditionally have called "blue-collar" jobs.

Still, the Supersites are worth trying (particularly if the job you are looking for is one likely to be found there). I don't think you should *only* use the Supersites, nor should you spend more than 5 percent of your job-hunting time there. The "extras" that they have for helping job-hunters are, for the most part, done better at sites like Job-Hunt, JobStar, and the Riley Guide. Also, many of the extras on the Supersites will cost you money, where the same services and quality (if not better) may be found elsewhere for free. But occasionally you will find gems on the Supersites, and it is also possible that they will work perfectly for you. Just go there—like everywhere else on the Internet—with your eyes wide open.

## Monster

**www.monster.com**

Arguably the best-known of all the job-hunting sites on the Internet, Monster has hundreds of thousands of job listings from all over the United States. Besides allowing you to search these listings by keyword, geographic area, and industry, Monster also has a Job Search Agent—a software program that will examine new listings as they are created and will email you potential jobs that match your criteria. In a few test searches, without regard to location, I found more than 5,000 listings for registered nurses, 2,600 positions for electronic technicians, more than 1,200 listings for truck drivers (though most were just ads from truck-driving schools), and 4 positions for cabinetmakers. There were 70 nationwide positions for research biologists and more than 5,000 positions for CPAs.

Monster offers many other services for the job-hunter—networking, newsletters, articles, and so on—though as I said, most of these extras are done better at the gateway sites.

Monster's basic services are free to the job-hunter, although you must register; it is funded by employers' job listings and by online advertisers (with some pop-up ads). Much of what is good about Monster has to do with its size alone, but give it its due: it is a well-thought-out and well-designed job site.

## Yahoo! HotJobs

**http://hotjobs.yahoo.com**
**http://hotjobs.yahoo.com/careertools**

This is not the largest of the Supersites by far, but it offers a better-than-average selection of articles and links to resources for job-hunters, including information on salaries, resume writing, interviewing, and relocating. Although there are some for-fee services scattered among the links, most of the stuff here is free.

In my brief sampling of jobs in this database, I found more than a thousand postings each for nurses and CPAs (when returning results, the HotJobs search engine is not specific about numbers over one thousand), thirty-two for electronics techs, none for research biologists, and ninety for cabinetmakers. Generally speaking, HotJobs seems to have a lower ratio of false ads than most Supersites. As with the other Supersites, employers are charged to list their job openings or to search resumes, whereas services are free to the job-hunter once you register. (HotJobs doesn't seem to have any mechanism for culling out old accounts and user names, so you might have to go through the registration page a few times before you find a user name that has never been used at one time or another.)

HotJobs brings Yahoo!'s resources and experience to the table in the community and networking arena. For example, you will see a list of professions—legal, telecommunications, government, health care, accounting and finance, the list goes on—inviting you to join in discussions with people seeking work in these various fields. As with all such chat facilities, you need to choose what you read carefully; there is a lot of complaining here. But that aside, there is still information to be gained and contacts to be made.

## America's Job Bank

**www.ajb.dni.us/**

This site, sponsored by the Department of Labor, has been closed since July 2007; the reasons why are somewhat vague, though I suspect it has much to do with budgets and competition from Monster and CareerBuilder. The other parts of the government's career resources still exist, though: these are America's Career InfoNet, CareerOneStop, and America's Service Locator. Going to the URL shown here will no doubt allow access to those websites for years to come—and because this is the federal government, the Job Bank may someday reappear, depending on the way Washington's political winds are blowing. For now, you are offered links to the various state-sponsored job sites.

### CareerBuilder

**www.careerbuilder.com**

CareerBuilder is owned jointly by the Tribune Company, Gannett, and Knight-Ridder—newspaper companies all. This means not only that it accepts paid postings from employers, but also that the database has want ads from around two hundred newspapers across the country. As a result, the database is huge, and because of the newspaper origin of many of the postings, you will find more lower-tech and traditionally blue-collar jobs listed here. In my unscientific sampling, I found 25 positions for cabinetmakers, 3,300 for truck drivers (again, most were ads), close to 22,000 for registered nurses (I suspect many are not actual jobs, but are from agencies and recruiters), 980 for electronic techs, more than 5,000 for CPAs, and 87 for research biologists.

Registering with the site allows you to search its database by keyword, field, and location; the site offers newsletters and other services. Because of its newspaper background, this site also partners with websites that offer apartment rentals, autos for sale, and networking (through Tribe.net) across the country. You can sign up to receive emailed information about career fairs in your area as well as for the *Cool Jobs* newsletter, which highlights certain jobs and companies that use CareerBuilder for hiring.

This site is more commercially oriented than the other Supersites, and there are certainly more pop-up ads. I was struck by the Resources page; the vast majority of links on the page lead to a fee-based offer rather than to the more typical free internet resource.

## THE JOB SEARCH ENGINES

When the Web first got going, it didn't take long before there was too much there for the average user to even know about. So the search engine was invented—a computer program that cruises web pages and uses a software tool called a "crawler" or "spider" to build a searchable index of what it finds. General search engines like Google and Yahoo! are known to everyone who uses the Internet, and I'll explore them in more depth in chapter 6.

But there are also specialized search engines, and in the last few years some have sprung up that are job oriented. So rather than having to go visit all of the different job boards on the Web, you can instead use a job-oriented search engine. Plug in the terms you want it to search for—computer programmer, engineer, nurse, and so on—and it will give you a list of any matching job listings it found on the sites that it is programmed to visit and index. What a huge time savings! Now you don't have to go, one by one, to all of the Supersites, career pages, and the thousands of specialized job boards on the Web; the job search engine will do it all for you.

Or will it? While all of the search engines listed in this section will indicate where each of its job listings came from, you have no way of knowing what job boards and career sites the search engine either does *not* visit or indexes incompletely. Just as with general search engines, the owner of a web page can stop a search engine from indexing what is on the site. So if, for example, Monster does not want SimplyHired to list the job postings on the Monster site, you won't get to see them when SimplyHired returns your search results. That wouldn't be so bad, as long as you *knew* that Monster was excluded. But the search engines won't usually tell you which sites they are and are not indexing; you must infer it. Furthermore, they may have their own rules about what they want to index on the various sites. So what you may get is a partial return of what is on different job sites, while you think you are getting everything. That's a problem.

Still, these search engines have a very wide reach; and they are so easy to use, it seems silly to not give them a try. Here are the best ones:

## Indeed

**www.indeed.com**

Indeed is one of the more popular job search engines. According to the site, its crawler searches "major job boards, newspapers, associations and company career pages," giving you a large database of job listings to look through. It allows you to browse through job listings by state and by industry field. You also get access to salary and job trends in various fields, and forums dealing with various fields and jobs. The site allows you to download plug-ins that integrate Indeed's job search functions into your web browser, and you can be alerted by email whenever a new job in your field of interest arrives. In their forum, you can read success stories from people who found jobs through Indeed.

Indeed accepts paid job listings directly from employers as well, on a pay-per-click basis. I think this is a bit unfortunate; it makes the site more (or less) than a straight search engine and inevitably leads to bogus job postings from recruiters, agencies, and companies that sell services to job-hunters. On the other hand, at least their "sponsored jobs" are well defined, just as any search engine's sponsored results are. Like everything on the Internet, perfection is elusive.

## JobMaps

**http://jobmaps.us/**

JobMaps is a combination of the Indeed job search engine and Google Maps. Input a job title and a city or state (this also works with "US" for the entire country) and you'll get a map showing where Indeed's listings for that job title are located.

## SimplyHired

**www.simplyhired.com**

SimplyHired is another good job search engine, with a very likeable interface. Their database represents close to five million jobs culled from "job boards, company pages, online classifieds and other data sources." In addition to searching, you can also browse listings by geographical area, job title, and field. You can view jobs by company, as they link directly to a number of company sites: Best Buy, Pepsi, Johnson & Johnson, just to name a few. It's fun to browse the listings and see where they came from; I'm a tad disappointed that SimplyHired gets so many of its jobs from CareerBuilder, which is my least favorite of the Supersites, but this may simply be a statistical indication of how many listings CareerBuilder has—it's hard to know.

SimplyHired is meshed with LinkedIn, the well known networking site (see chapter 4), so when a listing pops up at a certain company, you can find out with the press of a button if your LinkedIn network includes anyone at that company.

Finally, in the same way that SimplyHired allows you to access many job boards with a single search, you can also post your resume on a number of job boards by using their posting page. Checkboxes allow you to specify what sites you will post on. All in all, an excellent site, well worth your time.

## Jobster

**www.jobster.com**

Jobster is kind of halfway between a job board and a search engine. The site's crawler indexes jobs from the standard sites: CareerBuilder, Yahoo! HotJobs, Dice, and so on, as well as a variety of regional and specialty boards, and they also accept listings directly from employers.

The site encourages job-hunters to register and create a profile on the site. Your profile may contain your primary skills and other data; you can also upload video resumes and link your profile to, say, your personal website or MySpace page.

# 2. RESUMES

**I want to remind** you of two points I made in the last chapter, when I was talking about various job-hunting methods and their average success rates:

- It will improve your odds of job-hunting success if you use more than one method (but no more than three).
- It will improve your odds of job-hunting success if you introduce your resume as late in the job-hunting process as possible.

## MULTIPLE METHODS

Because it is to your advantage to use a variety of job-hunting approaches, the next decision you must make is to choose which approaches you will use. Obviously, it makes sense to use methods that have higher success rates. But maybe I should temper that a little bit: if you choose multiple methods that are all labor intensive, you may quickly find yourself bogged down, making very slow progress.

Some job-hunting methods may have low average success rates but are quickly accomplished. For example, using a job search engine like Indeed or SimplyHired is a statistically low-return method, but it takes so little time to do, you may as well give it a quick try at some point.

For the same reason, you might want to go to some job boards and post your resume. It doesn't take much time, and you might get lucky and have your dream job fall in your lap. Just remember that once you have tried SimplyHired or posted your resume on Monster, it is not time to take a break and call it a day; you are simply getting the low-return, low-effort methods out of the way so you can turn your attention to more effective job-hunting methods. In no event should you be spending a majority of your job-hunting time on these low-return approaches.

Once the statistically less-successful approaches are out of the way, what is left for most people is to do the following:

- Contact everyone you know, and anyone they can recommend, and ask them about possible job openings, places to work, new fields to consider, and so on. The common term these days is *networking*, and it is covered more fully in chapter 4.

- Inventory your skills and know which ones you most enjoy using. Do some research on what fields and job titles use these skills. Since skills are transferable between fields, it may be that you can explore new, fertile areas for employment that you had not considered before. Online methods of skill assessment are covered in chapter 5.

- Research companies, fields, and people with the power to hire you. Do research on salaries for various fields and geographical areas. Find out which companies are the best to work for, which companies pay better, and which have the best work environment. This kind of research is what the Internet does best, and it is discussed in chapter 6.

It may be beneficial at this point for you to write out your resume. This doesn't mean that you have to use it right now. But writing your resume is a good way of clarifying in your mind which skills you like best and want to use in your next job. Also, if you decide to post your resume on any job sites, I guess it would help if you had a resume to post.

# YOUR RESUME

What is the purpose of a resume? Traditionally, its primary purpose has been simply to get invited for an interview. It is not the best way, or the only way, of getting such an invitation. For example, if you know someone at the company you are interested in, their recommendation could get you that interview as well (and probably before any resume-generated interviews the company grants). In many cases, the best use of your resume is when you leave it with a prospective employer after your initial interview with him, as a reminder of you and your qualifications.

But we all know that most people don't use it that way. Instead, they use it to try and get an employer interested in them. In the pre-Internet days, it was not unusual for a job-hunter to send out hundreds of resumes, often without getting a single interview for a job. Now that we have email and all of the other benefits of the Internet, many employers are bombarded with thousands of unsolicited resumes daily; they have no choice but to treat them as nothing but spam. It's further proof of my point that you should not lead with your resume.

But at some point in this job-hunting process, you will need to prepare your resume. Depending on what approach (or approaches) you have decided to take, the best time for that may be now.

One of the most useful things you can do when you are writing your resume is to think like an employer. Here you are, struggling under an avalanche of resumes. You want to hire someone with certain qualifications and at least a minimum amount of experience at doing what you are hiring them to do. It would be nice if you could just go through this big stack of, say, a hundred resumes and pick the one that shines most brightly—but that isn't how it usually works.

In the first place, you, as an employer, are well aware that a resume is not the same as a person. What you really want to do is examine the people behind the resumes. But you don't have time to schedule a hundred interviews, so instead, you invite them all to send you their resumes. It's been done this way for many years.

But then there is the next problem. Very few people can read through a stack of a hundred resumes and remember which candidate had the best training, the most experience, went to the best school, and so on. Instead, what you want to do is make this stack of resumes *smaller. If I could just get this down to ten people—heck, five would be even better—then I could invite those people in for an interview.* And so you pick up the first resume and quickly read it. (The average resume gets a scan of, on average, eight seconds; rarely more than thirty.) At this point, you are not looking for the best candidate. Instead, you are looking for any little thing that will give you an excuse to throw this resume away so you can go on to the next one. In reality, you are not searching for the five best candidates. You are trying to throw out ninety-five resumes—*Survivor* meets the job hunt.

As a job-hunter, then, your mission is to write a resume that will survive this process. As you are writing your resume, you should constantly ask yourself if what you are putting in is necessary and on point. Most experts will tell you to leave out any information about your family, your hobbies, the name of your dog, who your third-grade teacher was, and so on. Account for employment gaps; leave out any personal data that might trigger someone's hidden prejudices regarding age, race, or religion; and of course make sure there are no grammar or spelling errors.

## RESUME TYPES

There are two basic ways you can approach writing a resume. The traditional method is to provide a chronological history of your work experience. This type of resume is best when you have no large employment gaps, you are staying in pretty much the same field that you have been working in, and the job you are now applying for is a logical step for you to make, considering your work history.

Another type of resume is generally known as the *skills-based* or *functional* resume. This allows you to present yourself in terms of your skills rather than as a person with a certain work history. This type of resume is best when you are changing careers or work fields, when you have employment gaps, or when your past job titles do not reflect your true accomplishments and skill levels. Also, if you are just entering or reentering the work force, you may want to emphasize skills from hobbies or volunteer work; this format allows you to do that.

A variation on this type is what Susan Ireland refers to as an *achievement resume.* Rather than listing your past jobs in terms of the duties you performed, you list what your achievements were at the positions you held.

Regardless of the format, your resume must at least survive the employer's initial perusal. If there is nothing immediately apparent that triggers the employer's desire to toss yours aside, the next thing that the employer is looking for is whether your qualifications fit the ones that have been established for the position in question. To meet this, many experts suggest that you tailor your resume for each position you are applying for, highlighting your skills, education, and experience that fit with the job's stated requirements.

I have mixed feelings about this, for a number of reasons. For one thing, what do you do when you are applying to the same employer for a number of different positions over a period of time? They could end up with very different versions of your resume on file; this could be embarrassing. It also would take excellent record keeping on your part to know which version of your resume has been sent to which employers when.

I think it is much better to have a single resume. This should be one page in length if possible—never more than two—and should emphasize the skills you most enjoy using. When you list your work history, depend less on job titles and more on responsibilities and accomplishments. If applicable, state in concise terms where goals were reached and deadlines met. Send this same resume to everyone. Then, if you are applying for a position where you feel that it would be helpful, include a cover letter that highlights how your particular skills and experience make you the best candidate for the job in question.

Finally, remember that employers are generally examining a job candidate's resume for three things: ability, experience, and attitude. Your resume and cover letter should convey these in the most positive manner possible.

## KEYWORDS

What computers do quicker than people, if not better, is to say that *this* thing is the same as *that* thing, or that the two are different, and then take some action based on that sameness or difference. This action—the *conditional branch*—is the essence of *all* computer programming, and the technology is well suited to seeing if a resume matches a job posting, or, more specifically, to seeing if the *keywords* in a resume match the keywords in a job posting. It's not the same thing.

These days, rather than struggling to make sure that your online resume contains all of the proper keywords you want it to have, without losing its readability, it has become standard practice to place a line or two at the end of a resume intended for online submission, headed by the term "Keywords:" and followed by a series of words, separated by commas, that are designed solely to trigger the search engine when an employer enters his search terms. This way, readability and grammar are no longer a problem. Just make sure that the series of keywords are all reasonable terms, given your skills and experience. You should try and limit the keywords to no more than two lines. I would also say that the keywords line is the one exception to the "Don't change your resume for each position you are applying for" rule. If you want to tweak the keywords a little bit to make sure that your resume is chosen, or rated a bit higher, that would probably be all right.

## RESUME FORMATS AND EMAIL

According to internet career expert Peter Weddle, fully half of all employers now prefer to receive resumes online. So once you have written your resume, you will need to have two versions of it. The content remains the same; it's the format that varies. One of your resume versions will be very nice-looking, well formatted, and printed on quality paper with a laser printer. This version is one you will, when applicable, send by U.S. mail (or similar) or hand personally to a prospective employer.

The other version of your resume will be one formatted for email. This one should look good as well, but it should be formatted in Courier monospace 12-point type, sixty-five characters to a line. This will allow you to send it as an email, or paste it into the majority of those employers' web pages that accept resumes. Instructions for converting your resume, using Microsoft Word, are available at:

Creating an Internet Resume

**www.job-hunt.org/internetresume.shtml**

This email-ready version should be sent to prospective employers, by email, when requested. Don't ever send your resume as an email attachment unless you are specifically requested to do so. Reference the job you are applying for in the subject line, and you should usually preface your resume with a short paragraph or two indicating any previous conversations, by phone or email, about the job you are applying for.

Finally, career expert Martin Kimeldorf advises adding something like this to the end of your email resume: "An attractive and fully formatted hard copy version of this document is available upon request."

## ONLINE ARTICLES ABOUT RESUMES

Speaking of advice, there is a huge amount of advice available on the Internet when it comes to the subject of resumes. I think this is because it is the one area of the job hunt that people feel most defeated about. Instead of realizing how flawed the lead-with-your-resume approach is, they say, "I'm sending out my resume; I'm posting it everywhere, yet I get no interviews. I guess my resume must be flawed." And in their frustration (gradually turning to desperation), they are willing to do anything . . . including spending money, maybe a lot of it. This has not escaped the notice of people who make their living in the resume industry; and you will notice that on many resume sites, the commercial temperature rises considerably.

Many sites on the Internet are a mix of commercial offers and free resources. You should never feel bad about taking advantage of such free resources, even when you have no intention of ever purchasing something at a site. Generally, the sites' owners put up the free resources to attract people to the site; they know that a certain percentage will become paying customers. This is a financial model used throughout the Web.

On the resume sites, you will have to wade through more than the usual number of offers for books, audiotapes, or whatever. And of course, the materials offered for sale contain the two (or maybe it's seven; I forget) secrets *that you absolutely must know* in order to achieve job-hunting success. You may be doomed to failure if you don't order today!

My advice to you is to live without these secrets if you are going to have to pay for them. There is so much free info about resumes on the Web, there's a chance you'll stumble on those five (or was it eight?) secrets to success anyway. If you spend the requisite time and effort at this on your own and eventually come to believe you need more assistance, then you can always purchase later.

Also, as you read through the resume-oriented web pages I will list shortly, you'll see that there is a great deal of advice and information, much of it contradictory. You should have only one resume; no, you should tailor your resume to every job you apply for. You should post your resume on as many sites as possible; *wrong*, you shouldn't send your resume unless asked to. You should use keywords; you shouldn't use keywords. You should refresh your resume on the job boards every few days, so employers will think it's current; ooooh, no, don't do that—and on it goes.

It is a sad comment on our job-hunting "system" that even the experts don't always agree on many aspects of job-hunting strategy; the subject of resumes is no exception. If you are confronted with contradictory advice, then just do what makes the most sense to you. After all, this is your job hunt, and your life; that means that, in the end, *you* are the expert and final arbiter. If a strategy works for you, that automatically becomes the best strategy to use; if it consistently fails, it is the worst, and to be avoided in the future.

That said, let's look at what advice you'll find online about resumes and cover letters:

### JobStar Central

**www.jobstar.org/tools/resume/index.cfm**

This site features excellent information (and links to more of same) about writing resumes for internet consumption. There are links to sample resumes, and the subject of cover letters is also, um, covered.

### CareerJournal Resumes

**www.careerjournal.com/jobhunting/resumes**

From the masters of business at the *Wall Street Journal*'s CareerJournal, here's a series of articles pertaining to resumes. Most are short and to the point; you will need to read a number of them to get the big picture, but the picture is there.

### ProvenResumes.com

**www.provenresumes.com/toc.html**

This site, based on Regina Pontow's *Proven Resumes* (Ten Speed Press, 1999) book, offers some very helpful articles about resume writing. The commercial temperature of the site is a bit higher than I would like, but the data here makes weaving through the site worth it.

### Susan Ireland Resume Writing Guide

**www.susanireland.com/resumeguide/index.html**

Good advice on resume writing, with many samples.

### Career Development eManual: Resumes and Cover Letters

**www.cdm.uwaterloo.ca/step4_2.asp**

From the Career Center at the University of Waterloo in Ontario, Canada, comes this section on resumes and cover letters. Leans a bit toward the graduating college student—it is a school, after all—but excellent all the same.

### How to Write a Resume Masterpiece

**www.rockportinstitute.com/resumes.html**

An article from the Rockport website. I particularly like the page with "power words" that you can incorporate.

## Creative Job Search Online Guide: Resumes

**www.deed.state.mn.us/cjs/resume.htm**

In the job search manual from Minnesota's Department of Employment and Economic Development, there is a good set of guidelines for resume writing, with excellent sample resumes.

## CareerLab: The First and Best Cover Letters

**www.careerlab.com/letters/default.htm**

Turning from resumes to cover letters, here's a collection of them available for free. There are cover letters galore, cold-call letters, thank-you letters, and letters helping you to leave a job gracefully, negotiate a pay raise, and so on.

## Cover Letters

**www.career.vt.edu/JOBSEARC/coversamples.htm**

From the Career Services office at Virginia Tech comes this excellent article on cover letters, with samples of same, including email versions.

## Resume Writer's Forum

**www.bestresumewriters.com/forums/index.php**

This site offers lots of resume samples and discussion about resume writing. A pretty good resource.

## Resume Resources for Job-Seekers

**www.quintcareers.com/resres.html**

From the Quintessential Careers site, a (long) list of (good) resume articles.

## Tips on Resume Writing

**www.montana.edu/careers/students/tips.htm**

This is not an article in itself, but a page of links to other sources, most of which are quite good.

## 15 Tips for Writing Winning Resumes

**www.questcareer.com/tips.htm**

Okay, so it was fifteen. Nice little article.

WetFeet Resumes

**www.wetfeet.com/Article%20Types/Resumes.aspx**

On this page is a list of resume articles. Each examines one facet of writing a resume and associated activities; most are very helpful.

## FOR-FEE RESUME SERVICES $$

**http://dir.yahoo.com/Business_and_Economy/Shopping_and_Services/Employment/Resume_Services**

**http://directory.google.com/Top/Business/Employment/Resumes_and_Portfolios**

Reduced to tears at the thought of having to write your own cover letter and resume (electronic or otherwise), even with all these aids online? If you are determined to go this route, and the services offered on the websites I have listed don't grab you, then there are a few hundred more for-fee resume and cover letter services in these two directories.

How do you evaluate who's good and who's not? Ask to see samples of resumes that actually resulted in jobs for their clients. Ask to talk to the client to confirm that this is so. Some resume writers will balk at this request; good ones won't.

## POSTING YOUR RESUME

Once you have written your resume, you are free to post it on the job boards and industry forums. But should you? You are releasing it into the public domain, where you no longer have any control about what happens to it. Recruiters and agencies can take it and use it for their own purposes; their best interests are not always yours. Information in your resume can be used for everything from annoying emails to outright identity theft. It's even possible that it can stay out in cyberspace for months, recirculated by various recruiters and agencies, only to pop up after you have landed a new job, causing your new employer to think you are still job-hunting!

And yet, people do this all the time; and sometimes—four times out of a hundred, on average—it actually works. So of course you can just go to the Supersites or use the job search engines to post your resume and hope for the best. But to increase your chances of success, consider doing some research on posting sites. Look for other job-hunters who found jobs this way. Consider going to forums and mailing lists in the fields that interest you and find out where (if anywhere) others have had success posting their resumes, and then follow their advice. Look at the job boards in chapter 3 and concentrate on job boards that cater to your field and your geographical area.

## PORTFOLIOS

An alternative to the written resume is a pictorial resume, often called a *portfolio*. It's not just pretty pictures; it offers proof that you have the skills you claim to have. Certain professions are known for using a portfolio (artists, models, craftsmen, and so on). But in the '80s and '90s, under the influence of books by career experts Eugene Williams, Martin Kimeldorf, and others, the idea was expanded to include many other types of work.

### Teacher Tap—Electronic Portfolios

**www.eduscapes.com/tap/topic82.htm**

This is a good place to start. The accent is on the digital or multimedia portfolio, but there are many links on many different portfolio aspects.

### Portfolio Library

**http://amby.com/kimeldorf/portfolio**

Here Martin Kimeldorf describes in great detail his view of what a portfolio can be—the why, the wherefore, and the how-to. His form is not by any means the only way to go—it's long and directed at educational situations—but it may stimulate your own creativity.

### Portfolio Basics

**www.bsu.edu/students/careers/documents/portfoli/**

Ball State University's Career Center outlines the basics of portfolio development, what should be included, and so on.

### Portfolios.com

**www.portfolios.com**

On this website, you can post your portfolio as part of a searchable database. There are also links to other sites that deal with creative talent. People looking to hire creative people post job listings on the site as well.

## PERSONAL WEB PAGES

Some resume experts recommend an HTML-based resume for those in computer graphics, programming, web development, and similar fields. It's not a big step from that to setting up your own personal web page when you are job-hunting, and pointing prospective employers there.

Before going this route, make sure you are doing this for good sound reasons: are you convinced it will improve your chances of finding a job? If the answer is yes, then make sure that your job-hunting web page is as businesslike and straightforward as possible: no extraneous personal information; no pictures of your kids, the family dog, or your Puerto Vallarta vacation. And never forget that once you put things up on the Internet, you lose a certain degree of control over what happens to such information.

If you have considerable experience with computers, you might want to set up the site yourself, or you can hire someone to do it for you. One of the best places to find such people is craigslist (**www.craigslist.org**).

An alternative to setting up a personal web page, and somewhat simpler besides, is setting up a page on MySpace. This is not a typical thing for the average job-hunter to do (yet), but for young people, and particularly people in music and the arts, uses for MySpace are expanding all the time. For example, though it started as simply a social networking site just a few years ago, it is now considered a handicap for people in the music and related industries to *not* have a MySpace page. A few more years may see the same sort of thing for other industries as well—maybe yours.

## How Do I Set Up a Website?

**www.boutell.com/newfaq/creating/setup.html**

To learn the basics of setting up a website, start here. This site assumes you know almost nothing and explains it all well, without trying to sell you something.

## Tips for Setting Up Your Website

**www.microsoft.com/smallbusiness/online/web-hosting/articles/tips_for_setting_up_your_web_site_and_email_accounts.mspx**

Speaking of trying to sell you something, this site does a good job of explaining the basics of setting up a website, but the commercial temperature is set pretty high: ignore the heavy push to buy Microsoft products and services.

## Creating Your First Website

**www.adobe.com/devnet/dreamweaver/articles/first_website_pt1.html**

If you have access to Dreamweaver—a popular web-page development program from Adobe—this site explains in simple terms how to create the actual pages of your website, using that program.

## GoDaddy

**www.godaddy.com**

Even though their television commercials are somewhat tasteless—they are available on the GoDaddy site if you don't believe me—GoDaddy is one of the most popular and least expensive web-hosting services available. They have lots of resources to help you design and build web pages.

## MySpace

**www.MySpace.com**

The famous site. By the way, did you know that MySpace has job listings posted in their Classified section?

# 3. THE JOB BOARDS

**One of the reasons** that the Supersites—Monster, CareerBuilder, HotJobs—have such a poor success rate for most job-hunters is that they are victims of their own success. They have shown themselves to be excellent at pulling in job-hunters and storing their resumes, but as time passes, fewer employers are going to the Supersites.

This is partly because of resume smog. Monster's database has forty times as many resumes as job listings. The Supersites have become very popular destinations for online job-hunters, and employers often find themselves inundated with hundreds—even thousands—of resumes for a single job opening. And many of these are just "resume spam," without the qualifications the job requires. (Employers call this "noise in the database.") A recent survey of six major employers showed that for every one hundred job openings filled, fewer than one of their hires came from Monster. For CareerBuilder and HotJobs, the percentage was even lower: between two and four of every thousand hires. Imagine the time the employers wasted looking through resumes—in many cases, *thousands* of them.

So employers are turning away from the Supersites. And if the employers aren't going there, it doesn't make much sense for the job-hunters to go there; they should go where the employers are going! So . . . where *are* the employers going?

Well, there are some clues. In 2005, the WEDDLE's consulting firm surveyed 3,900 recruiters and human resources personnel. Of these, only 11 percent said that they would be using "general recruitment" websites; 84 percent said that they preferred to use the niche job boards and avoid the Supersites.

Similarly, the Herman Trend Alert says studies indicate that more job-seekers get jobs through niche job sites than through the general ones. By choosing the job boards that target their industry and/or geographic area, job-hunters feel they are more likely to deal with real jobs at real companies, and the employers are subject to far less resume smog.

So: the employers prefer the smaller sites, and the job-hunters prefer the smaller sites. Sounds like a win-win situation, doesn't it? Except for the fact that job boards in general—large or small—still do not have a very good success rate for the average job-hunter.

Well, you may not be an average job-hunter. It may be that a regional or specialty job board will have just the job you are looking for, and you may be exactly what the employer listing there needs. As long as you don't spend an inordinate amount of your job-hunting time doing it, it makes sense to visit some of the smaller job boards appropriate to your situation.

## ARTICLES ABOUT JOB BOARDS

Before you start visiting the job boards, it might be a good idea to read some articles about them. The following articles should help you with formulating an approach to using the job boards more effectively:

### Using Web Job Sites

**www.job-hunt.org/jobsearchusing.shtml**

### Keeping Track of Your Job Search

**www.job-hunt.org/jobsearchtracking.shtml**

### The Dirty Dozen Online Job Search Mistakes

**www.job-hunt.org/jobsearchmistakes.shtml**

A triumvirate of excellent articles from Susan Joyce at Job-Hunt.

# REGIONAL JOB SITES

This is just a small sampling of some regional job boards. Later in this chapter, I list web pages that have links to hundreds more.

Also, you can go to any search engine and try doing a search on "[your city or area] job board" or "[your city or area] jobs" and see what comes up. More and more, newspapers in the larger cities are running their own internet job boards; and craigslist, which has a huge number of localized sites, is always excellent.

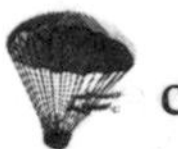

## craigslist

**www.craigslist.org**

Started in San Francisco, craigslist has spread around the United States and the world. Though more of a community bulletin board than your typical job board, craigslist is a site you ignore at your peril when job-hunting. Why? Because there are *tons* of jobs here. As well as the typical range of jobs, there are others here that may interest you, particularly if you are looking for a job with a smaller business, if your work is more creative than most, or if you want to tap into areas of employment that might be somewhat out of the mainstream. Additionally, if you are starving and need some quick hourly or by-the-job work, the "gigs" section can be a life-saver—or an apartment-saver, or a car-payment maker.

Also, it is interesting to note that craigslist is at least partly responsible for the growing dissatisfaction with the Supersites. Check out the page at **www.craigslist.org/about/job.boards.html**, which compares the effectiveness, cost, and responses generated for ads placed on craigslist and the three most popular Supersites.

## RegionalHelpWanted.com

**http://regionalhelpwanted.com/corporate/our_sites_usa.cfm**

Most people have never heard of Regional Help Wanted. But many *have* heard of "Bay Area Help Wanted dot com" or "Help Wanted Phoenix dot com" or "Central Illinois Help Wanted dot com" and so on—hundreds of them in the United States and Canada. Using the standard fee-to-employer, free-to-job-hunter model, the site's innovative radio ad campaign has helped to establish Regional Help Wanted across the country in record time.

Job-hunters can click on the map at the page listed here or go to the alphabetical city listing at **http://regionalhelpwanted.com/corporate/our_sites.cfm** and find the nearest one (the map will clearly indicate areas without a local board). Once there, you will find a better-than-average job board with very complete job descriptions (there's effectively no limit on the number of words employers can use to describe a job listing). The ratio of jobs available to job-seekers registered varies widely and wildly from one board to another in the system; you should check and see what's available in your area.

### JobDig

**www.jobdig.com**

This is the website of a popular (and free) job newspaper of the same name, which publishes weekly regional issues for cities in Minnesota, Wisconsin, Iowa, Nebraska, Kansas, Oklahoma, and the Dakotas. Currently headquartered in Minneapolis, they are expanding into other markets. The website lists many jobs for the covered areas—you can search for a job by location, job type, or employer—and the on-site employer directory is a neat feature. You can also view the various regional issues of the paper online; these contain helpful articles by well-known experts in the work and job-hunting fields, as well as the published job listings and employer ads.

### BostonWorks

**http://jobs.boston.com/careers/jobsearch**

A regional job board for the Boston area, sponsored by the *Boston Globe*.

### *Washington Post* Job Board

**www.washingtonpost.com/wl/jobs/home**

A regional job board for the Washington, D.C., area.

### Jobing.com

**http://colorado.jobing.com/default.asp**

A regional job board for Colorado.

## THE NETWORKED SITES

At the risk of sounding repetitious, there are many thousands of job-hunting sites on the Web (the accepted figure in the industry is forty thousand, but how accurate that figure is, or where it came from, I have no idea . . . I think it's kind of like "Don't eat with your elbows on the table"; everyone said it, but no one could ever tell me, *Why not?*). Although few of the databases for these many job boards are identical, there are many that are similar.

Here's why: most websites that want to offer job-hunting services to their clientele can't, because there's no good way to begin. Without a database of resumes and job listings to start with, they can't attract employers and job-hunters to their site to post their resumes and job listings. They need something to jump-start the process before they can attract enough employers and job-hunters to their sites to build up their databases to a useful level.

A number of companies have leaped in to offer just such a jump-start package to these sites: kind of a "job board in a box." Just add website, job-hunters, and employers. A number of companies offer this kind of core database and software package; examples are CareerBuilder, BestJobsUSA, and Beyond. A niche site using one of these services will, naturally, add new listings and resumes from and for its special clientele, which will tend to make its database somewhat unique to its site, but many listings are shared among sites as well.

Although I have listed a variety of job boards in this chapter, I have made no effort to try to list even all of the good ones; there are just too many. If you click around to a number of them, you will start seeing the similarities and differences that identify the primary networked sites.

Along with the sites listed, look at the directories of job boards; there could easily be a special job board for your field with job listings that might be found only there. But use your common sense: you don't have the time to sign up at a hundred different job sites, and it's unlikely that doing so would substantially raise your employment prospects.

## Beyond

**www.beyond.com**

It isn't the best; it's certainly not the worst. Beyond is typical of many job sites on the Web, and for a very good reason: it *is* many of the job sites on the Web. Besides hosting a network of well over a thousand specialized job boards, it provides software for industry associations and similar organizations that want to have a job board on their website. Go to **www.beyond.com/network/** for links to their member and client job sites. You should visit it just because its network is so extensive.

### JobBank USA

**www.jobbankusa.com/search.html**

With job-hunting resources and articles at the site, as well as the standard database of job postings, JobBank USA is pretty typical of most boards. What the site lists as a metasearch function is mostly a hosting function for other websites that have job listings, such as newspaper and niche boards. As is typical with this software, the search agent cuts a pretty wide swath; a search for "registered nurse" positions yielded, among other things, a posting for a patent attorney. Hmmm. Maybe one with a funny hat.

Anyway, the site is not bug free, but it does have a kind of personality; check it out and see what you think.

## COLLEGE AND GRADUATE SITES

### CollegeGrad.com

**www.collegegrad.com**

I love this site. There is no better one available on the Internet for the college student or recent graduate. Excellent resources, good job database, with all the features such a site should have. Well done, Brian Krueger.

### CollegeJournal

**www.collegejournal.com**

Another of the *Wall Street Journal*'s many arms, this one is as professional as the others. Good database, better than average resources.

### AfterCollege

**www.aftercollege.com**

Focuses on internships and entry-level and summer jobs.

### CollegeRecruiter.com

**www.collegerecruiter.com**

Entry-level jobs and internships.

# NICHE, TRADE, AND SPECIALTY SITES

There are about a bazillion niche job boards—I should know; it feels like I've been to every one of them. Here is what amounts to only a sampling of what is available for various trades, industries, and professions. I have tried not to list the sites that are part of the major job-site networks, preferring instead to find job boards that are independently operated and well thought of in their particular industry; I have not always been successful.

Note that I have not attempted to be complete or fair. As the mother hen said to her chick while pointing out an ostrich egg, I just want you to see the possibilities. If these aren't enough, and you want to find more job boards in your area of expertise or interest, go to a search engine and type in "[some profession] jobs," of course substituting your area of interest for "some profession." A list will come up of sites for you to try.

## Job Spider—Employment Resources Directory

**www.thejobspider.com/job/directory/employment-resources.asp**

A really good directory with all kinds of employment resources. Excellent for finding niche job boards.

## FindLaw

**http://careers.findlaw.com**

The best of the legal job sites, in my opinion. A good database with law jobs of every description, from judge through summer associate, office manager, law librarian, even temps, all searchable by location and area of specialty. Outplacement resources, suggestions for nonmainstream legal positions—there's even a section where us nonlawyers can find a nearby attorney who practices in the required specialty.

## LawJobs

**www.lawjobs.com**

In addition to its database of legal jobs for attorneys, paralegals, legal secretaries, and the like, the site also includes temp positions, employment trends, and other useful info for the job-seeker. As with most legal job sites, a quick look through its employer directory reveals that most jobs listed are through legal recruiting firms. What is true in many fields seems true in the legal profession as well: most jobs are found through networking.

## Legal Career Center Network

**www.thelccn.com**

Not accessible to the average person (or book writer), this is a service that is offered through various professional organizations. Check with your local bar, paralegal, or legal assistant association to see if it offers access to members.

## EmplawyerNet $$

**www.emplawyernet.com**

Unlike most job sites, EmplawyerNet charges the job-hunter and is free to the employer. EmplawyerNet.com charges $125 a year to access its database of legal jobs.

On the plus side, the site does have a free directory of legal recruiters and employers around the country, grouped by city and state. Because so many law jobs are through recruiters anyway, you might skip the fee and go straight to the recruiter list, using the site as a research source only.

## TrueCareers

**www.truecareers.com**

Though TrueCareers bills itself as a job board for "degreed professionals"—and its database does indeed include listings for civil engineer, Java developer, senior tax associate, architect, airport engineer, and so forth, there are also listings (and ads mixed with listings, of course) for delivery drivers and salesmen—really smart ones, I guess.

But most of the positions are for what I think of as high trades—engineering, accounting, project management—like that. Pop-up ads are incessant and very persistent.

## BioSpace

**www.biospace.com/jobs**

The Career Center page of this biotechnology website, with the standard industry-oriented job and resume databases, is searchable by location, salary, company, and specialty. An interesting little tool is the Job Assessor, with which you can rate the different aspects of two possible jobs, side by side, and then come up with a final score to indicate the more desirable.

## StyleCareers

**www.stylecareers.com**

A job board for people in the fashion industry: apparel, footwear, home fashion, beauty, textiles. Actual positions run the fullest possible range: hair stylist to photographer to purchasing agent to color specialist to makeup artist . . .

## AllRetailJobs.com

**www.allretailjobs.com**

The name kind of says it all, doesn't it?

## Creative Hotlist

**http://creativehotlist.com/index.asp**

A job board for people in the creative arts, such as photographers, graphic artists, art directors, and artists of every stripe. When you register, you receive a URL on the site that points prospective employers straight to your profile, with your personal data and links to any examples of your work that you've posted. An interesting feature is that you can post portfolios as well as resumes (the cost is $35 for six months; everything else on the site is free). A neat site.

## Jobs for PhDs

**http://jobs.phds.org**

As job boards go, this one is pretty quirky; I guess it reflects the personality of a lot of those PhD types (maybe I should have listed it under "Diversity"?).

## MedHunters

**www.medhunters.com**

Health-care jobs—more than eleven thousand at last count—are listed here; a superior site. One of the nice touches is that it groups jobs so that you can browse by lifestyle, such as sun, mountains, coastal, exotic, major sports nearby, rural and small town—neat, huh?

## Jobscience

**www.jobscience.com**

Another good health-care niche board.

## HealthCareersUSA.com

**www.healthcareersusa.com**

Part of the BestJobsUSA network, this site specializes in, obviously, jobs in the health industry. I haven't listed too many of the BestJobsUSA sites; I find the software buggy and aspects of the database are incomplete. But there are a number of sites in their net, so it might be worth checking.

## The Blue Line

**www.theblueline.com**

Law enforcement, fire, and civilian law (dispatcher and so on) positions.

## Groovejob

**www.groovejob.com**

A job board for teenagers; the focus is mostly on hourly and part-time positions.

## Jobs in Trucks

**www.jobsintrucks.com**

A job board for trucking and transportation jobs. Be careful—a significant number of the postings are really bait being dangled by truck-driving schools.

## Job Kite

**www.jobkite.com**

This job board specializes in jobs in small business. It is better than many of the cookie-cutter job boards that litter the Internet; there is also a humor section, which is refreshing to see.

## ComputerJobs.com

**www.computerjobs.com/homepage.aspx**

Tech jobs of all descriptions are available through this site. A number of excellent features are here; for example, you can list the number of jobs available in various cities, list jobs by various specialties and skills, and click on a city to see the jobs available in that city, sorted by specialty. My latest visit showed almost ten thousand job listings, of which a quarter were less than a week old (an excellent currency rate for an internet job board) and what at least *appears* to be proof that these jobs are getting filled.

## Computerwork.com

**http://computerwork.com**

Another good job site for the IT professional. Decent-size database, all of the features of the better job boards, plus a few extra features, including a special link for reporting outdated jobs in the database—surprisingly rare.

## Chemjobs

**www.chemjobs.net**

Chemistry and engineering job board.

## Workforce 50

**www.workforce50.com**

A very unusual niche board in that it lists jobs for seniors. Granted, there aren't a huge number of jobs in the database, but it's nice to see that someone is thinking about this part of the population.

## Work in Sports

**www.workinsports.com/home.asp**

A job board for people interested in sports careers.

## Construction Jobs

**www.constructionjobs.com**

A well-designed job board for the construction, design, and building industries. More than just a job-listing and resume database, the site has helpful articles and resources for the job hunter. In some cases, you can apply directly through the website for jobs that interest you—a feature that is becoming increasingly popular at many job boards.

## Mechanical, Electrical, Plumbing Jobs

**www.mepatwork.com**

MEP Jobs is a job board for those seeking jobs in the trades, such as HVAC, plumbing, electrical, and so on. The database is a shared one and it contains an unfortunately low number of actual trades jobs.

## Dice

**www.dice.com**

Long a popular board for people in the tech industries, as well as author of various IT industry and salary reports, Dice has recently expanded its database to include jobs in biotech, aerospace, and engineering. During my last visit, it claimed to have more than fifty thousand current job listings; that's a lot of jobs. Dice's database serves as the core for a number of other tech job sites.

## EmploymentGuide.com

**www.employmentguide.com**

Kind of a job board for everyman: beauticians, carpet cleaners, handymen, delivery drivers—like that. It gives links to other, more specialized boards for certain niche areas, like health care. Annoyingly, but not unusually, some ads are mixed in with the job listings.

Like reading the classifieds in the newspaper, sometimes you just need to see what jobs are available in your area before you even know what job titles you should search for; that's why I like it when job boards allow you to browse through all of the available jobs in your area. EmploymentGuide lets you do just that, with the names of employers included—a nice feature.

## AutoJobs.com

**www.autojobs.com**

A job board for those in the automobile industry. Most of the jobs listed are in support industries, such as dealerships and repair facilities, but there are also jobs grouped under manufacturers, management, and aftermarket manufacturing, as well as under sales, sales management, body shop, technician, service, and office personnel.

## HCareers

**www.hcareers.com**

Many companies have turned to the Internet for hiring, and the service industry is certainly no different. Wal-Mart. Taco Bell. Circuit City. Marriott. Blockbuster. Hilton. Red Lobster. At the HCareers site (actually, a group of three sites), you'll find hospitality, restaurant, and retail jobs—more than forty thousand of them. You can search by management or nonmanagement, type of business, area, and so forth. There are links to overseas service jobs as well. An *excellent* site.

## SHRM Jobs

**http://shrm.org/jobs**

From the Society for Human Resource Management, this job board is for people in the human resources field: payroll, benefits analysts, recruiters, HR managers and personnel, and so on. A nice feature is the Between Gigs forum and bulletin board, where you can talk and share job leads with others.

## jobsinthemoney.com

**www.jobsinthemoney.com**

Loan officer, accountant, finance manager, tax analyst. If you are looking for a job in the finance industry, this is a good place to start.

## Medzilla

**http://medzilla.com**

A job board for pharmaceutical, biotech, science, and health-care jobs. This one is a website with character—I like the design. You can search the job listings or browse the employer database to see what's available.

## ServeNet

**http://servenet.org/Organizations/BrowseJobOpportunities/tabid/295/Default.aspx**

From the ServeNet site, this is a list of current job openings with nonprofit or social-conscience organizations.

## Teachers Support Network

**www.teacherssupportnetwork.com**

A job-hunting site for teachers. Services are free, though you must register. I list this as part of my "no teacher left behind" philosophy.

## Chronicle Careers—Careers in Higher Education

**http://chronicle.com/jobs**

From the *Chronicle of Higher Education* comes this really excellent job site. At my last visit, there were jobs in its database from almost 1,100 institutions of higher learning, with openings all across the spectrum, from university president to tenured posts to lab assistant to groundskeeper. Resources include advice on how to turn your CV into a resume, salary calculators, web links related to academic careers, and a forum for discussing these and other subjects. Top-notch.

## Jobs for Librarians

**www.lisjobs.com**

A job site for librarian and information professionals. Job listings are current, browsable, and searchable. There is also salary information for librarians, links to industry articles, and job-hunting advice. An email newsletter is available, and there are even links to overseas jobs in the profession.

## EntertainmentCareers.Net

**www.entertainmentcareers.net**

A job board for those in film, television, and live theater, listing a huge range of jobs in broadcasting, television news (if you ever doubted that TV news was primarily entertainment, look where they advertise their job openings), production, film studios, theaters, and so on.

## Idealist

**www.idealist.org/career.html**

Jobs and internships in public service and nonprofits.

## Telecommuting Jobs

**www.tjobs.com**

Jobs that involve telecommuting or work at home.

## The Write Jobs

**www.writejobs.com**

A job board for writers.

## Technical Writers Jobs

**http://tc.eserver.org/dir/Careers/Job-Listings**

Not a job board itself, but a page of websites catering to jobs for technical writers and those in the professional, scientific, and technical communications fields.

## DIVERSITY

### LatPro

**www.latpro.com**

The "essential job board for Latino and bilingual professionals," this is the best of the diversity job boards, with excellent resources and an extremely large database. LatPro's high visibility attracts a lot of employers, which attracts many job-hunters, which attracts a lot of employers, which . . .

### HireDiversity.com

**www.hirediversity.com**

Another excellent site. Good database, with articles and resources for African Americans, Asian Americans, Hispanics, disabled people, gays and lesbians, mature workers, veterans, and women.

## WOMEN

### Women For Hire

**www.womenforhire.com**

A job board specifically for women, obviously; the database looks similar to that of other job boards I have seen, and I doubt that the employers in the database were advertising only for women; that would be worrisome. It's more like the site is woman-friendly, with articles aimed at helping the working woman and mother.

### Career Women

**www.careerwomen.com**

One of the leading women's boards.

### Women's Job List

**www.womensjoblist.com**

A job board for women that also partners with other job boards and employers.

# PEOPLE WITH DISABILITIES

## disABLED person/RecruitABILITY

**www.disabledperson.com/recruitABILITY/js.htm**

This site provides a resume- and job-posting service, targeted toward people with disabilities and employers who are sensitive to their needs. The service is free to both job-hunter and employer.

## WORK*ink*

**www.workink.com**

A Canadian site designed for job-hunters with disabilities. There are job- and resume-posting services and other resources. It has an extensive—and very current—listing of jobs for those with disabilities on the site. Access is, of course, free.

# GOVERNMENT JOB SITES

## Federal Jobs Digest

**www.jobsfed.com**

You can browse this site's job listings by state and county or look through its occupational groupings. Search categories include salary, location, and job grouping.

## USAJobs

**www.usajobs.opm.gov**

This is one of the U.S. government's official sites for jobs and employment information. It is absolutely current and at the time of writing contains almost seventeen thousand jobs. But this is by no means all of the jobs available with the federal government; many agencies use their own hiring resources, and you won't always find such jobs listed here.

## FedWorld Federal Jobs Search

**www.fedworld.gov/jobs/jobsearch.html**

Another federal jobs site with a pretty similar database to USAJobs but possibly better search tools here.

## CONTRACT AND TEMPORARY JOB SITES

There is a big difference between private employment services—"headhunters," "executive search," and the like—and temporary agencies. For many unemployed people, temp agencies are a godsend. And there are times when temporary positions work their way into full-time positions as well; careers have started this way.

### Net Temps

**www.nettemps.com**

This site is excellent. Thousands of temp, contract, and permanent jobs; excellent articles and resources for the job-hunter; good links to other resources. Most of the jobs are current and appear legitimate (recruiters often put in bogus jobs to try to sign up the desperate). If temp work is what you want (or need, for now), give this site a try.

### American Staffing Association

**www.americanstaffing.net/jobseekers/find_company.cfm**

Best way to find a temp agency on the Internet. Indicate your area and the kind of work you want, and it kicks back a list—sometimes a very extensive list—of temp agencies near you.

### The Employment Guide

**www.employmentguide.com**

Specializing in hourly and part-time jobs.

### SummerJobs.com Location Search

**www.summerjobs.com/jobSeekers/index.html**

### ResortJobs.com

**www.resortjobs.com**

### InternJobs.com

**www.internjobs.com**

### OverseasJobs.com

**www.overseasjobs.com**

These four sites are part of a network of job sites for "students, recent graduates, expatriates, and adventure seekers." Job openings around the world, primarily aimed at young people and the service industry. As is typical, the search agent cuts a broad swath, but the sites are good, nonetheless; great links pages, too.

### Cool Works

**www.coolworks.com**

Links to thousands of jobs in national parks, resorts, cruises, camps, ski resorts, as well as ranch jobs and volunteering.

### SnagAJob

**www.snagajob.com**

Part-time, restaurant, hourly, summer jobs; listings, resources, guidance, advice. Youth oriented, but not exclusively.

### Backdoorjobs.com

**www.backdoorjobs.com**

Summer situations and temporary, outdoor, and overseas jobs are listed. This is the website for *The Back Door Guide to Short-Term Job Adventures* (Ten Speed Press, 2005).

### ContractJobHunter $$

**www.cjhunter.com**

A job board for contract and consulting work; access will cost you a minimum of $25 per year, though you can search the employer database for free.

## EXECUTIVE JOB SITES

### 6FigureJobs

**www.6figurejobs.com**

The premier site for executive positions, top rated by everyone who does that sort of thing. Maybe a tad more commercial than the average job board.

### ExecSearches.com

**www.execsearches.com**

A job board for executive and senior-level positions with "nonprofits, public sector, and socially responsible businesses." The Registry is its service that emails you with matching job postings.

### CareerJournal

**www.careerjournal.com**

Mentioned often in this book as an excellent resource site, the *Wall Street Journal*'s careers website also has a job and resume database. Positions tend to be management and upper level, as you would expect.

### Construction Executive

**www.constructionexecutive.com**

This is a job site for executives in the architecture, construction, and engineering industries, as well as related manufacturing industries (steel, piping, wire, and other building products, and heavy equipment, for example).

### ExecuNet $$

**www.execunet.com**

Well rated, but as with all such things online and off, research carefully why this particular service or site is different, better, and necessary before you plunk down that credit card. Memberships start at $150 for ninety days.

## INTERNATIONAL

### Best Jobs

**www.bestjobsus.com**

This is the U.S. site in a series of sites with job postings from various countries. The database is not the most extensive, but it's not an area for which extensive listings are often found. The jobs that are here are searchable and browsable (nice feature) by location, industry, and how recent the listing is. Many jobs are shared among the various sites and are listed as "overseas." The site does have a lot to recommend it. I particularly like the data on the employers in the database, which lets you look at individual employers in a variety of ways, see how many employers are in which cities and states, and see how many positions each employer has listed on the site. Here are the websites for the other countries in the network:

Australia **www.bestjobsau.com**
Canada **www.bestjobsca.com**
Hong Kong **www.bestjobshk.com**
India **www.bestjobsindia.com**
Indonesia **www.bestjobsid.com**
Ireland **www.bestjobsie.com**
Kenya **www.bestjobske.com**
Malaysia **www.bestjobsmy.com**
New Zealand **www.bestjobs.co.nz**
Philippines **www.bestjobsph.com**
Singapore **www.bestjobssg.com**
South Africa **www.bestjobsza.com**
United Kingdom **www.bestjobsuk.com**

## Seek

**www.seek.com.au/**
**www.seek.co.nz/**
**www.seek.com.au/uk/**

Based in Australia, with a strong presence in New Zealand (and also expanding into the United Kingdom), Seek is an excellent job board. Well organized, with many resources for the job-hunter; the employer database is also extremely useful and well implemented. On the UK site, there are even resources for those moving to the British Isles, with information on taxes, transferring funds, housing, and so forth. Very well done.

## Job Databases

**www.jobdatabases.co.uk/**

On this page you will find links to all kinds of online job sites based in the United Kingdom. In addition to employment agencies, recruitment and human resources firms, and links to specialized sites (jobs for the disabled, degreed placement, and so on), there are links to hundreds of job boards that specialize in special fields and various areas of the United Kingdom.

## Guardian Jobs

**http://jobs.guardian.co.uk/**

Another good UK site. One very nice feature is the employer database (a feature I think that *every* job board should have). Employers in their database are listed alphabetically along with the positions that firm has recently advertised or filled.

## Workopolis

**www.workopolis.com/index.html**

This is a Canadian job site that is partnered with (and its ownership situation is very similar to) CareerBuilder here in the States. I would wager it has similar benefits and liabilities. There are better-than-average resources here for the job-hunter, including Bob Rosner's "Working Wounded" column. If you are looking for a Canadian job, this might be a good place to start.

## Jobsite

**www.jobsite.co.uk/home/advsearch.html**

A UK site with jobs in the United Kingdom (of course), Europe, and the Middle East. Not necessarily a lot in every country—as few as thirteen vacancies listed, for some, when last visited.

## Eurojobs

**www.eurojobs.com**

Has listings for jobs in a surprising number of countries; you can search by standard keywords and location or browse jobs by country. Currently not as large a database as one might hope.

## Australia's Careers OnLine

**www.careersonline.com.au/menu.html**

A pretty good job board, regardless of the area it serves. The jobs database is for Australian jobs, of course, but there's a good, if slightly small, collection of resources here for everyone. I particularly like the Job Seeker's Workshop, a map for online job-hunting.

# VOLUNTEERING

There are a number of reasons to volunteer:

- It can be a route toward a paid position at an organization, whereby you can demonstrate your skills and value to the organization without straining its limited payroll resources.
- It can be a good thing to do if you are currently unemployed or waiting for a new job to start and you have time on your hands that you don't need to spend job-hunting. Helping others is much better, karma-wise, than watching *Jerry Springer*.
- Because networking is the quickest route to a new job, this is one more way to increase the number and range of people that you know, who may be able to help you find work.

If volunteering seems like something you would like to do, whatever your reasons, then here are some sites to try:

## VolunteerMatch

**www.volunteermatch.org**

A good site for finding programs in your area. Mentoring, community projects, outreach to the elderly, local library book drives, neighborhood food banks—the list is endless. It even has a Virtual Volunteer section, where you can, for instance, donate your time to animal rights, conservation, and philanthropic organizations that need web designers, grant writers, artists, and so on. A *very* good site.

## ServeNet

**www.servenet.org**

Another volunteer site, also with quite a few listings. This site is somewhat more polished than VolunteerMatch. It has resources like tip sheets for volunteers, articles about volunteering, news clips, and the current temperature, which is always important to know whenever you get the urge to help somebody. The site has a lot to recommend it, including sections on virtual volunteering, a listing of jobs for pay currently open at nonprofits and social-conscience organizations, newsletters you can sign up for—there's quite a bit here.

### National Park Service—Volunteering

**www.nps.gov/volunteer/**

This is where the National Park Service posts information about internships, employment, and volunteering opportunities.

### Volunteer Canada

**www.volunteer.ca/index-eng.php**

This is a government-funded website for volunteering in Canada. It's more of a clearinghouse for information than an actual place to look for volunteering opportunities. To volunteer, you link up with one of the two hundred volunteer centers (well, okay, *centres*) across Canada at **www.volunteer.ca/volcan/eng/content/vol-centres/locations_new.php**.

### Global Volunteer Network

**www.volunteer.org.nz/programs**

This site, too, is more of an information clearinghouse for various programs around the world than a site for placing volunteers in such programs. Accent is on overseas programs in depressed areas.

### WorldVolunteerWeb.org

**www.worldvolunteerweb.org**

This is the site created by the United Nations to serve as a center for information, organizations, and programs related to volunteering on a global basis. This site is best for getting a worldview of volunteering in general; if you are looking for hands-on situations, then the other sites listed here are more likely to be useful to you.

## LINKS TO JOB BOARDS

There are thousands of job boards that I haven't listed. To find them, try going to these pages to see what else is available:

### U.C. Berkeley—Job Listing Sites

**http://career.berkeley.edu/Infolab/JobSites.stm**

A good list of niche job boards and other resources.

## Riley Guide—Job Banks and Recruiting Sites

**http://rileyguide.com/multiple.html**

A truly great list from Mary Ellen Mort of niche boards and recruiting sites, arranged alphabetically.

## Job-Hunt—Local Resources

**www.job-hunt.org/state_unemployment_offices.shtml**

This part of Susan Joyce's excellent gateway site lists local job-hunt resources for all fifty states, as well as websites of local employers and all of the state employment offices (see the State Employment Offices section listed later in this chapter).

## Beyond/4Jobs

**www.beyond.com/network/**
**www.4jobs.com/MKT/Content/Network.asp**

As mentioned earlier, Beyond (formerly, and to some extent still, known as 4Jobs) serves as the core for hundreds—maybe even for more than a thousand—job sites. Many of these are niche or international sites, and the databases can vary from one to another, even though a lot of the listed jobs will be common to all. At any rate, this page contains a list of, and links to, all of the sites that are part of the 4Jobs network. It's an impressive list.

## Online Recruitment Magazine

**www.onrec.com/content2/boards.asp**

Online Recruitment Magazine has a database of job boards—over four thousand, last I looked—organized by country and field. Go to this page to find them.

## Academic360.com

**www.academic360.com**

Links to many resources for those seeking a job in academia. Good site.

## Open Directory Project

**http://dmoz.org/Business/Employment/Job_Search**

From the Open Directory Project, this is a directory of career sites on the Internet. If you are looking for a niche site that may be somewhat obscure, this directory is likely to have it.

### Jobs for the Disabled at Careers.Org

**www.careers.org/jobs/01-55-diversity-employment-disabled.html**

A very good list of links for job-hunters with disabilities.

### Usenet

**www.jobbankusa.com/newsgrou.html**

I don't think that there is much future in using Usenet for disseminating job openings, and I don't think you should ever post your resume this way. But if you want to cover all bases, here is a list of job-listing newsgroups. You can count on almost any jobs found this way to be either IT-oriented, academic, or extremely specialized.

## AFTER THE JOB BOARDS

At this point, you have visited some job boards, maybe posted your resume, and set things up so you'll be notified if that perfect job listing comes in. And while you're waiting, we should probably look at some of the other low-return job-hunting strategies that I mentioned back in chapter 1. These include answering newspaper ads, going to your local unemployment office, and visiting private employment agencies.

## NEWSPAPER HELP WANTED ADS

News flash: the newspaper help wanted ad, as we have known it for generations, is disappearing.

It's not hard to see why. For years, newspapers have seen declining readership as more people turn to television for its version of the news. And now, with the growth of the Internet, more people are going online for news as well and not buying newspapers.

For now, almost all newspapers put their content online without charge. But it costs money to go out and gather news. While people are turning to these free online news sources, they probably don't realize that these online sources get their content from the print newspapers that fewer and fewer people are buying. It is not a healthy financial model, and it cannot last forever. Online ad sales are insufficient to support a professional newsgathering staff. Not long ago, the *San Francisco Chronicle* had to lay off one-fourth of its news staff, and other papers in the Bay Area have been the subject of mergers or buyouts in the last few years. The same trend is seen in other parts of the country as well.

One effect of this is that newspapers are trying to save money wherever they can, and one way is to outsource their employment want ads to Yahoo!, CareerBuilder, and similar organizations. You may find that there is not much difference between what is in your newspaper's want ads and what is available online by the outsourcer.

Employers know this too—so if they are going to place an ad, often they will skip the paper and go directly to the online job boards. This may be a Supersite, or they may go with a more local touch. So if you are going to check the local newspaper want ads, you should probably also check the regional online job boards for your area.

### Refdesk—Newspapers USA and Worldwide

**www.refdesk.com/paper.html**

An index to the websites of thousands of newspapers around the country, organized by state, and around the world, organized by continent and country.

### American Journalism Review NewsLink

**http://newslink.org/daynews.html**

Another site where you can find links to more than four thousand newspapers, grouped by city and state. The site also has listings of radio and TV stations, magazines, and international publications. An absolute gem.

## STATE EMPLOYMENT OFFICES

We used to call this the "unemployment office," but the sign outside never says that anymore. It will say "Employment Development" or "Department of Employment Security" or something like that. But regardless of the name, if you have been laid off, you may have already been there to register for your unemployment check.

The job listings tend to be low-wage and low-responsibility positions, though there are exceptions. For example, many state, local, and municipal government jobs (including positions in school districts and park and recreation entities) are required by statute to be listed with the local unemployment . . . oops, I mean, employment development offices. As long as this is not the sum total of your job-hunting efforts, it is probably worth your time to poke your nose in and see what is available. (Such nose-poking can often be done online.)

### U.S. State Employment Offices

**www.careers.org/topic/01-20-jobs-listed-at-state-job-services.html**

A directory of the employment offices in the fifty states. Interesting how many different names the various states have come up with to call these offices—probably so you don't feel so *unemployed*.

### Career InfoNet—Newspapers and State Employment Services

**www.acinet.org/acinet/crl/library.aspx?PostVal=10&CATID=21**

A list, organized by state, of local newspapers and state employment offices, as well as a selection of other local resources helpful to the job-hunter.

## PRIVATE EMPLOYMENT AGENCIES

The subject of private employment agencies—often called "employment consultants," "executive search firms," "executive placement," or something similar—is a difficult one. Many people feel drawn to these places out of either ignorance or frustration. This makes them ripe for plucking by unscrupulous people. It is unfortunate that these agencies have been the greatest source of consumer complaints related to job-hunting.

When people hold themselves out as professionals, we pay them because they know things that we don't—how to fix a broken water pipe, what drug to take when we are sick, how to defend a lawsuit or rebuild a transmission. It is seductive to think that you can just write somebody a check and they will find a job for you while you are fishing or watching TV or whatever you would rather be doing (anything!) than job-hunting.

But nobody can do your job hunt for you; the best they can do is help and guide you. With very few exceptions, private employment agencies don't know anything that you don't or couldn't know with a bit of research. If you are drawn in their direction, make sure that they really have something to offer you that you cannot find elsewhere.

There are essentially two kinds of private employment agencies: ones that you pay and ones that the employer pays. Try to stay away from the first kind. Their success rate is usually extremely poor, and they are not in the habit of refunding your money. The second kind are of the "headhunter" or "executive search" variety and tend to work with high-level executives who are worth the employer's paying someone to find. If you are not one of those executives, you will be wasting their time, and after numerous rejections you will probably end up with a firm that charges you.

Regardless of who pays, research prospective firms thoroughly. Get recommendations. Look for satisfied customers. If you can't find any, maybe that's, like, a clue? Don't even consider going to a particular firm unless it is recommended by a number of people in situations similar to yours.

### Executive Search Firm Database

**www.searchfirm.com/search/search.asp**

This database has an excellent search function, allowing you to look for firms by specialty, method of payment, and so forth. There are some good resources on the site as well.

### Riley Guide—A Short List of Search Firms

**www.rileyguide.com/firms.html#list**

A list of firms from Margaret Dikel's excellent site.

### Bernard Haldane: Busting the Bad Boys

**www.asktheheadhunter.com/teeth20031013.htm**

An article about business practices at one of the largest private agencies in the United States.

Beware of Employment Scams

**www.bbb.org/alerts/article.asp?ID=269**

An article from the Better Business Bureau.

Critical Tips for Job Seekers to Avoid Job Scams

**www.worldprivacyforum.org/jobscamtipspayforwarding.html**

## HOWEVER . . .

Do note the difference between private employment agencies, as just discussed, and those that deal with temporary job placement. "Temp" agencies, like the ones listed in the Contract and Temporary Job Sites section earlier in the chapter, can be quite useful, especially if your job hunt is lasting longer than your savings.

And of course there is a huge difference between private employment agencies or employment "consultants" (often the same thing in disguise) and real career counselors. If you are having trouble with your search for work, there is nothing wrong with paying a competent, experienced career counselor to advise you, on an hourly basis, about how to conduct your job search efficiently—more on this in chapter 5.

# 4. CONTACTS AND NETWORKING

**Now that we have** looked at some of the less effective ways of job-hunting online, let's start taking a look at the more effective ways. Unfortunately for those of us who would prefer a magical solution, the more effective methods take a more active approach; which is to say, more work on your part.

However, there's a payoff for your effort: not only will these methods tend to get you a job faster, but the job you end up with is more likely to be the job you want, using the skills you most enjoy, and offering greater rewards—not the least of these being an increased salary. Moreover, the contacts you make, and the skills you develop while you work at your online job hunt, will be of the sort that are very much in demand these days and will serve you well in the future. So let's take a look at the next step in the job hunt: networking.

People love to talk. We are social animals. If people can't talk to each other face to face, then they will invent other ways to talk to each other—hence the telephone. And when actual talking is impractical or impossible, they will find other ways of "talking": facial expressions, smoke signals, telegraphy, traffic lights, graffiti, letter writing, sign language, texting, and hand signals (especially while driving!). And of course, people do the same thing on the Internet, using bulletin boards, email, chat rooms, usenet groups, and websites, many of which are specifically set up for nothing but talking. And all of this works to the job-hunter's advantage.

Job-hunting is people hunting. An employer is looking for a person who will do the work he needs done. A job-hunter is looking for a person who will hire him. It usually takes a number of steps before they each find the person they are looking for.

So we can say that job-hunting is a search not only for information but also for people—for human links between you and information, between you and a prospective employer. These days, such links are called *contacts*, and a common word for all of your contacts is your "network." And, no surprise, we call the act of mining our list of people for information and contacts *networking*.

In the job hunt, networking is often the secret of the game. Consider: a 2003 study showed that for the companies participating, 60 percent of their new employees were hired through employee referrals or the Internet. Because other recent studies have shown that the Internet accounts for less than 10 percent of new hires, that leaves us with *half of the open jobs being filled through networking*. Other studies back up these numbers.

The quickest way to find a job is to have a friend tell you that they need someone exactly like you where he is currently working. It's rarely that easy, but if you don't *directly* know someone who can tell you of a job opening, then the next step is to see if any of your friends know of someone else who might be aware of an opening. Or maybe one of *their* friends do, and so on, extending further out away from you. And interestingly, the further out you go, the more likely you are to find a job this way, and it's not just because of the increasing number of people involved.

## THE STRENGTH OF WEAK TIES

The experts say that most of us know between 150 and 250 people. When they say that you "know" that many, they don't mean that you go out to dinner with that many or even have the home phone number of every one of them. But that's the number of people whom you can claim as friend, relative, or acquaintance—people you interact with, who would recognize your name. Within your circle of 250, there is your *core*: the few with whom you are especially close, along with maybe another twenty or thirty that you socialize with or see regularly. Outside of your core is the rest of your 250; these are the ones that you are obviously not as close to, like your wife's brother out in Oregon, that nice older woman in the accounting department, your sister's no-good kid.

It makes sense that the people you are closest to will have more in common with you; they will tend to have the same interests as you, and they will tend to know the same people as you—there is a lot of overlap between *your* circle of 250 and *their* circle of 250. And because of that overlap, they will be more likely to know what you know. And in the same way, *they* will be less likely to know what *you* don't know—in this case, of possible job openings.

It is when you start getting further away from your core, and start finding people with less overlap between your 250 and theirs, that you will find the people—and the information—that you and those closest to you are less likely to know. Though it seems paradoxical, it is the people that you know *least* well who are most likely to be helpful in your job hunt. This is called *the strength of weak ties*.

You cannot ignore this concept. To make your job hunt more successful, you need to find the people you do not know well, or at all. The *less* well you know them, the *more* helpful they are likely to be to you. And, lucky you, the Internet is pretty good at this.

## INTERNETWORKING

Before I offer some links to online articles about networking on the Internet, I'd like to point out that although networking is something the Internet does pretty well, there are very few good *online* articles about how to do it. There aren't even that many good offline articles about how to do it. What that says to me is that people are still learning how to use the Internet in this capacity; maybe it also says that not all people are comfortable with the whole concept of networking, in general, during their job hunt.

But even if that's true, it just means that this is an area that is ripe for innovation and new approaches. If you come up with an idea for how to do this better, that can only be to your benefit. Who knows? You might even have a new career ahead of you.

## CareerJournal Networking Articles

**www.careerjournal.com/jobhunting/networking/**

If you need to find out more about networking for your job hunt, this should be your first stop.

## Market Yourself Online

**www.infotoday.com/mls/oct01/gordon&nesbeitt.htm**

Although written for librarians, the principles involved are the same for pretty much everybody. The article discusses all of the things I have been talking about in this book: networking, resumes, personal websites, and so forth.

## Career Playbook: Job and Career Networking

**www.careerplaybook.com/guide/networking.asp**

Some good tips in this one.

## Informational Interviewing: A Networking Tool

**www.quintcareers.com/informational_interviewing.html**

Readers of *What Color Is Your Parachute?* will be familiar with the critical concept of the informational interview: meeting with someone whose interests are similar to yours and finding out what and whom they know that may assist you in your job hunt. Quintessential Careers' website has a good series of articles on how to do this properly.

## Networking Your Way to a New Job

**www.quintcareers.com/networking_guide.html**

Also from Quintessential Careers. Check the site thoroughly for more articles on this subject.

# FINDING PEOPLE ONLINE

Networking is all about people. Some of them you know; some of them you don't—yet. Even when you know them, you won't always know exactly where they are. Here are a number of tools for finding somebody when you have a basic idea of who it is you are looking for (and don't forget the resources for finding people in chapter 6):

## PeopleData

**www.peopledata.com**

There are a number of websites like PeopleData; essentially, they are phone book databases, often with hooks into other databases, such as Intelius, ZabaSearch, and ZoomInfo (see the following entries). This allows such sites to pull up birth dates, names of relatives, and so forth. It's a hook of a resource when you are trying to find someone—but doesn't all this worry you just a bit? I wonder about the world we are becoming, when everything about everyone is stored on thousands of computers around the world, and privacy is as rare as noble motives.

## ZabaSearch

**www.zabasearch.com**

This slightly scary website provides free address and contact information for names entered, at no charge. ZabaSearch does not use telephone-centric resources to look for people; nor does it do web scans like ZoomInfo. Rather, it uses "public records"—and for examples of what *that* means, see the following entry for Intelius.

## Intelius

**www.intelius.com**

Similar to ZabaSearch, Intelius's data comes from "utility records, court records, county records, change-of-address records, property records, business records, and other public and publicly available information." More detailed data is available for a price.

## ZoomInfo

**www.zoominfo.com**

This is actually a search engine oriented toward finding information about people. Pulling data from a number of resources, this site can come up with surprising results. Enter a name and you'll get a list of people and their business affiliations, sometimes going back for years (this is one instance in which outdated information on the Internet can be quite valuable). Click on the name for email address and other data.

Although the site asks you to sign up for their premium services, the free searches are still pretty good. You can search for an individual with or without a company affiliation, search for employees of a specific company, alumni of a specific school, or all the people mentioned on a specific website. ZoomInfo also has some other neat features, including a database of companies and industries, and a partnership with the job search engine Indeed.

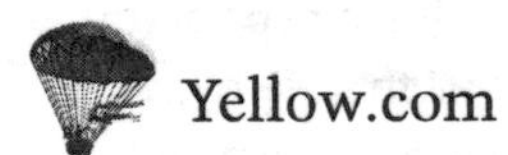

## Yellow.com

**www.yellow.com/white.html**

As well as being an excellent site for looking up businesses, this is also one of the best for finding people. From a single form, you can search the Yahoo!, WhitePages.com, Addresses.com, 411.com, and InfoUSA directory listings. There are also pages for doing reverse number lookups and address searches, along with a search for people who have a web presence. Also a zip and area code lookup database, with links to maps, services, and so on.

## InfoSpace

**www.infospace.com**

One of the best finders on the Internet, for people and businesses. In addition to having a very complete database, it boasts some neat features, including a metasearch engine that quickly samples Google, Yahoo!, Ask, and About.

## Email Search

**www.internet101.org/searching/finding-email-addresses/**

Websites to help you find people's email addresses. For the most part, I have not found sites like this to work very well, but I remain ever hopeful.

### Langenberg.com: PeopleFinder

**http://person.langenberg.com**

From a single page, this site allows you to access a number of people-finding resources: the Verizon White Pages, email address searches through Bigfoot and Yahoo!, alumni searches, professional associations, Usenet postings, obituaries (!), and the membership lists at MSN and ICQ.

I have to say that this is a good site, but it is not a great site. It would be a great site if all of the links worked as they should. But during the times I have tried it, some of the page's resources worked fine, while others were painfully slow, and still others just plain didn't work, period. So if you're striking out with the other sites listed here, give this one a try. Hey, this is the Internet; by tomorrow, the site could work perfectly, or it could be gone completely.

### Canada 411

**www.canada411.com**

People listings for Canada.

## FINDING PEOPLE AT THEIR BUSINESSES

If you need to locate someone's business, or their business's website, try these next few entries (many more tools for finding people and companies are available in chapter 6):

### Rutgers University Library—Biographical Resources

**www.libraries.rutgers.edu/rul/rr_gateway/research_guides/busi/biography.shtml**

If you want to find out more about the people you are looking for, try the resources listed on this page. Resources available here range widely: industry associations, membership directories, magazine articles, industry biographies, industry "Halls of Fame," encyclopedias of industry and business leaders—you get the idea.

### Vault

**http://vault.com/companies/searchcompanies.jsp**

A good site for locating companies; you can do a search using various parameters such as industry, city and state (and country), number of employees, and annual revenue.

## Business.com

**www.business.com**

This is essentially a business search engine. You can browse their large database of business categories as well.

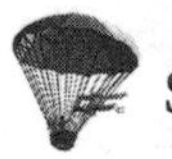

## Spoke

**www.spoke.com**

Spoke is a database of companies and people, with profiles of both. If you are looking for people to contact at a company you are interested in, this is an extremely useful site. The site was originally designed for sales contacts, but people have discovered ways to use its database that go far beyond that; naturally, that includes job-hunting contacts.

## Yahoo! Company Directories

**http://dir.yahoo.com/Business_and_Economy/Directories/Companies**

Another extensive directory, organized by industry—thousands of companies, with links to their home pages.

## WEDDLE's Professional Associations

**www.weddles.com/associations/business.htm**

Where are you likely to find those who are doing what you want to do? This is a terrific list of professional associations, from the site of one of the masters of the job hunt and the Web.

## Company and Military "Alumni" Networks

**www.job-hunt.org/employer_alumni_networking.shtml**

A great list of company alumni groups (many are from Yahoo! Groups, another good source), and a terrific resource when networking.

## U.S. Colleges and Universities

**www.utexas.edu/world/univ/**

The alumni organizations from the various colleges and universities are also terrific places to find contacts. Go to the individual websites to find the alumni groups.

### Alumni Services

**www.careerresource.net/alumni/**

An alphabetically organized list of links to alumni services at educational institutions. It's disappointing that this has not been updated since 2000, so some links will not work. Still, a little work with a search engine should help you bridge whatever gaps you find.

### CheckDomain.com

**www.checkdomain.com**

Maybe you don't know anybody at the company you are interested in, and you can't seem to come up with a contact there at all; nor do any of the standard business directories help. Assuming the company has a website, you can plug the company's website URL into CheckDomain's search engine. It looks through the database of domain registrations and returns basic data about the company, usually including an administrative contact. If it's a large company, the administrative contact may be the same as the technical contact, which may be just an IT manager or a trusted programmer in the IT department—but for smaller companies, you may have just gotten the name and contact info for the head guy, or somebody close to him.

When you get your search results, ignore the message about "This domain is taken"—of *course* it's taken; you knew that. The data you want is farther down.

### URL Investigator

**www.urlinvestigator.com**

Another way of tracking information about a company's website.

## MAKING NEW CONTACTS

The number of contacts you can make online is mind-boggling. Any faraway place that interests you, you'll likely find a contact online. Any question you need an answer to, you'll probably find someone online who knows the answer. Any organization where you need to meet the person with the power to hire, chances are you will find someone online who knows somebody who knows somebody . . .

And how do you find these people? The Internet has a number of tools for doing this. No single method works in all cases, but here are the basic ways of meeting people on the Internet.

## Chat Rooms

Chat rooms are places where you "meet" with other people, online, in real time, and talk with each other using your keyboards. It's like watching the dialogue from a play script unfold line by line on your screen. Chat rooms are found on commercial services such as America Online and MSN; on websites such as Yahoo! Chat; and at many hundreds (if not thousands) of special-interest websites, where people can chat about that site's specific subjects. Some job-hunting sites have chat facilities.

Generally, the chat sessions will be among a number of people—most sites allow any number of people to "listen" but may limit the number of people who can get in at any moment to "talk." Some of these will be moderated, meaning that there is someone in charge, watching over the conversation, with the power to disconnect those who behave badly. But in fact, these are rare; most sites require self-policing. Many sites allow you to search through past conversations by keyword, so be careful what you say; it may be stored somewhere for a very, very long time. Some chat sites will allow you to leave the main thread and "go off" to a private room for one-to-one conversations, but these are usually sites that lean toward personal relationships rather than business ones. In fact, of all of the ways you can meet and communicate with people, chat rooms are the *least* likely to be useful in your job hunt.

## Message Boards

Message boards—which, more and more these days, are being called *forums*—are similar to chat rooms except that the conversations do not occur in real time. They are more common than chat rooms and, for job-hunting purposes, far more useful—in fact, they can be absolute gold mines. They are found most often at websites devoted to a particular subject, field of interest, or function, such as magazines, industry or hobby sites, career sites, colleges, and so forth.

All forums will have a general subject or field of interest, usually related to the subject of the hosting website. For example, Ezine Articles is a website for writers; you can go to its message board at **www.ezinearticles.com/forums**. People use this area to discuss various aspects of writing.

Different parts of the forum are divided into subheadings within the field. You can think of these like rooms in a house, with each room dedicated to a specific area of the larger subject. At this site, there are rooms labeled Earning Money from Your Articles, Where Else to Promote Your Articles, Copywriting 101, Ghostwriting Questions and Answers, and so on. If you're interested in one of these more specific subheadings, you can click on the title for access to that "room."

Once you're in the room, you can read previous conversations—called "threads"—or start a thread by asking a question or making a statement for discussion. Anyone can read any thread, and those registered with the site (which is almost always free) can post a response to any thread. The response, officially called a *reply* (gee, there's a surprise), can occur almost instantaneously, or it might be years later, and all replies become a part of that particular thread. The thread itself belongs to, and stays in, the same subheading, or room, where it was started.

Some threads "die" without any replies or very few. Some threads generate multiple replies, replies to replies, and so on, and the thread can go on and on, sometimes for weeks, months, and occasionally years. At any time, multiple threads are active, and in theory all threads that have started since the birth of the board are active, though in practice threads do tend to die after a while from lack of attention. All threads, active or not, are always searchable, by subject, keyword, date of posting, name of person who posted, and so on. Which is to say, *everything* that has ever been said on this board is searchable, and accessible by anyone, *forever*. As a practical matter, you should limit your searches to specific time periods. If you go too far back in your search, you run the risk of retrieving outdated information, as well as data overload.

One of the things you will notice if you spend much time on message boards/forums is that certain people tend to post more often than others, and that others' replies to them will tend to be extra respectful and deferential. These are the people you should cultivate; they tend to be authorities. They know a lot about their subject and are generally familiar with other forum regulars. If you want to communicate with one of these people only, most message boards will allow you to send messages directly to that particular person; these are called *private messages*, or PMs. Private messages are not included in the board's database and are *not* searchable or viewable by others. This is how people exchange email addresses without exposing themselves to spammer harvesting bots and the general nuisances that sometimes hang around the boards.

If you spend time on message boards and get to know the people there, they can be *terrific* places for cultivating contacts. Just remember what Grandma used to say: you never get a second chance to make a first impression, and first impressions *really* count, especially when what you say is remembered forever. Before you say anything, do a *lot* of listening. Often, the people on these forums have been dealing with each other over an extended time period, and as with any group, newcomers are sometimes viewed warily. Most important, don't ask a question without doing a site search to see if the question has been asked in a previous thread. Failure to do this can make it difficult for you to gain acceptance—and may even open you to ridicule.

## Wikis

Wikis are collaborative websites to which a number of people can contribute. The best known is Wikipedia, which is a collaborative encyclopedia. Wikis are a great place to find people with common interests, as well as a certain amount of authority (or at least, one hopes, knowledge and competence) in their field.

If you are feeling a little skeptical about wikis as a place for finding contacts, take a minute and go to Wikipedia's Community Portal page (start at their main page at **http://en.wikipedia.org** and click on the Community Portal link) and just look at all of the projects, collaborations, and teams there are. This is a gold mine of contacts, united by common interests.

Wikipedia is not the only wiki on the Web; it's just the biggest. For other wikis, use a search engine; combine a field of interest with the term "wiki" and see what pops up. Also, check out Wikiversity, one of Wikipedia's companion sites, at **http://en.wikiversity.org/wiki/Wikiversity:Browse**. The site is less developed than Wikipedia at the moment, but that's not necessarily a bad thing for your purposes.

## Newsgroups

Newsgroups are very similar to message boards, except that whereas message boards are always found on the Web, newsgroups are from Usenet, a part of the Internet that predates the Web. Originally, newsgroups were used to spread news about their subjects; now there is no pretense of such a limitation, and you can find all kinds of things discussed and posted here.

Not all Internet service providers will give you Usenet access, and not all ISPs give you access to all of the possible groups. But Google has archived a large number of newsgroups and continues to do so. You can search and access these through your web browser, regardless of whether or not your ISP allows you Usenet access.

Usenet group names look like this: alt.subject.subheading. If you look at the parts of the name, separated by dots, you'll see that it's a *hierarchy*: the name starts out generally descriptive and gets more precise as you read from left to right, just like a website URL. With Usenet, they all start with a prefix, which gives you the general area—the *very* general area—of the group's subject of interest. There are thousands of hierarchies and group prefixes. Here are some of the more common ones:

**alt.** This used to mean *alternative*, as in "an alternative approach to" whatever-the-subject-in-the-rest-of-the-name-is. This was back in the days when the Internet was full of college kids and society's young rebels. Now, it more or less means "this group is about anything," because yesterday's rebels are today's bowling league and PTA.

**rec.** Subjects dealing with recreation

**comp.** Computer related

**sci.** Science

**soc.** Social and societal areas

**net.** Network or Internet related

For a complete list of all Usenet name hierarchies, go to **www.magma.ca/~leisen/mlnh/mlnhtables.html**. For more data on Usenet in general, go to **http://en.wikipedia.org/wiki/Usenet.**

All newsgroups are open to everyone with Usenet access. Because Usenet dates from the early days of the Internet, it remains a favorite part of the Internet for those people who know more about computers and the Internet than most of us; we might unkindly call them geeks or hackers. Newsgroup postings are in text only, and they lack the pretty formatting that you are used to seeing on the Web (as well as some of the message boards' abilities, like private messaging).

Overall, I would say that newsgroups are more likely to produce contacts and job-hunting information for academics or those in the information technology fields. If you are not in one of these areas, you may well do better to stay away from Usenet and stick with the other possibilities the Internet has to offer.

## Networking Websites

Networking websites are sites specifically set up for networking. Examples are LinkedIn, Facebook, MySpace, Tribe, and Monster Networking. Each is a bit different from the others, but all have been set up in acknowledgment of the power of networking in business (and other) relationships, job-hunting certainly not the least of these.

However—and it's a big however—although these sites are specifically meant for networking, they are not always the most *effective* approach to networking. Human beings are drawn to those who share their interests—people with whom they have something in common. At the business-networking sites, for example, there isn't really anything that the people all have in common, other than ambition and a desire to better their employment position in one way or another. Would you rather do a favor for a friend of a friend of a friend—in other words, someone you don't really know and don't really have anything in common with—or someone who shares your love of woodworking or gardening or working with disabled kids or what have you?

When you are networking, you will find greater success if you think of ways to connect with people who share your interests. These could be work-based interests—if you are a video game programmer, then find a chat room where video game people hang out—or they could be hobby-based interests. You could still be a video game programmer, but if you really like flying radio-controlled airplanes on the weekends, go to the RC chat rooms and make contacts there. You will be much more likely to find lasting relationships when there is something you genuinely have in common with people, especially when it touches your enthusiasms. These are the people who will really want to help you, far more than the father-in-law of your ex-brother-in-law's next-door neighbor. And you may be surprised how many programmers (or computer game company executives) like to fly model planes, too.

Another bond is that of common experience. Websites like Classmates and Corporate Alumni can yield good contacts because, in a sense, these are people you already "know" and with whom you have similar or shared experiences. College alumni, in particular, feel a sense of bonding toward their school's other graduates and are often happy to help. (On a smaller scale, the same principle extends to people who took the same night class that you did last year, or attended the same seminar or weekend retreat.)

## Mailing Lists

Mailing lists are similar to newsgroups but are done through email. There are mailing lists on every subject possible; you subscribe to the lists you want to receive by sending an email, and those lists are then sent to you periodically. If you want to stop subscribing, you send an "unsubscribe" message. (The subscription process is completely automated; I once had a heck of a time getting off some lists when the underlying software was incorrectly installed by the list manager, because there was no human to contact.) Like Usenet, mailing lists are another older Internet device. Many lists, at least the noncommercial ones, are disappearing. There are just better ways of communicating on the Internet these days.

Also, when compared to message boards and Usenet, mailing lists are a slow method of communicating, particularly for the job-hunter. Though at times useful for gathering information, they are not as immediate in their nature as the other possibilities on the Internet, so I would not recommend them for direct communication with others.

But listen well, dear reader: *every* resource on the Internet (and off) can always be used for contacts, data mining, and name gathering. Who are the authorities in the field? Who is it that others listen to? Who is respected and well known? What people write the bulk of the articles and periodicals in the field? Who are the people that others interview most? Quote most? (It is also valuable to note who are the ones that other people ignore.)

Generally, the people who are more highly placed in their field will be the ones who know the most people in their field. As a corollary to the "strength of weak ties" principle, the people that *they* know well will also tend to be more highly placed.

These people will, of course, tend to be busier than most, but they are no less approachable for that. Just remember that anyone you contact on the Internet (or off) should be approached respectfully, politely, courteously, and with keen awareness on your part that this is a busy person who may or may not be able to respond to you. If they do help you, you should always email a thank-you note, promptly, for the help they gave you.

# CHAT ROOMS

## Yahoo! Chat

**http://chat.yahoo.com**

Still the king of the nonsubscription chat room, Yahoo! has hosted chat groups for years, and thousands of people have used Yahoo! to increase the reach of their personal networks. Because it is so well known, it is one of the first places I would go for general chat subjects.

## AOL and MSN

**www.aol.com**
**www.msn.com**

Both of these services have extensive chat and messaging areas for members. You are, of course, limited to those who are members of that service, and such services are becoming increasingly irrelevant. Bear this in mind before you go rushing in.

# FORUMS AND MESSAGE BOARDS

Before I list places for you to go to access message boards, I should mention that in almost every case, the entries here would be second on my list of places to go. I think you are far more likely to make useful contacts at forums that are specifically related to the industry or field of interest that you are targeting for your job hunt; such forums will normally be found on the websites of industry magazines, associations, or even large companies in that field. Generally, you can locate these by using your favorite search engines and searching on something like "[name of industry] forum," "[subject] message board," or "[field of interest] discussion group"; use your imagination. Also, try searching lists of periodicals and industry magazines and newsletters, and then checking their websites.

Also, you can try these, in descending order of importance:

## BoardTracker

**www.boardtracker.com**

This is a pretty neat search engine. Enter a subject, and it will search through its database of forums and see if there is a thread that matches your subject. You can also go to the forum that was the source of the thread and look for more stuff that might interest you and make contacts thereby.

## BoardReader

**http://boardreader.com**

Boardreader is another search engine designed to find forums and message boards. It is not flawless, but it is often helpful.

## Big Boards

**http://directory.big-boards.com**

This is a directory of forums and message boards, organized by subject. They lean toward the large and popular forums; that may not be the best thing for you. But of the forum directories available on the Web, this is (as I write, at least) the most complete.

## Yahoo! Groups

**http://groups.yahoo.com**

They do everything else, why not this? Yahoo! has thousands of groups: industries, hobbies, personals, careers, . . . tons. If you look under Business and Finance, many of the groups you will find were created for networking in specific industries.

## HotJobs Communities

**www.hotjobs.com/htdocs/client/splash/communities/**

This is from Yahoo!'s career site; there are thirty-five industry-specific message boards accessible here.

# NEWSGROUPS

As I have mentioned already, you must be careful with Usenet newsgroups. Most of what is available is useless to you: people's opinions about this or that, flames (whereby someone is harshly ridiculed for having posted something others disagree with), bad data, old data, false data, worthless data—in a word, junk. But we are looking for people now, not valid data. You will be able to apply your own sense of truth to what you read, and you will soon know who knows their stuff and who doesn't. If you aren't clear about which is which (or who is who), try another part of the Internet where there is less data smog.

## Google Newsgroups

**http://groups.google.com**

Probably the best place to go these days to find newsgroups. The index is very easy to browse, the database is searchable, and it claims to have over a billion postings.

If you are unfamiliar with Usenet and/or Google, go to **http://groups.google.com/googlegroups/help.html** for answers to your basic questions about Google's groups and how to access them.

## Tile.Net

**http://tile.net/news**

I happen to love Tile.Net. No frills, nothing fancy, just *lots* of listings in various categories—in this case, thousands of newsgroups, organized by description, hierarchy, or name index. The Description category will usually be best for discovering groups; use the Index, when you know the group name you want. Clicking on a group takes you to a summary page; many of these summaries contain links to web or FTP documents where you can learn more about the subject and, of course, who wrote it. Aha, an authority! Not a bad place to start.

Clicking on the group from the summary page will cause your newsreader client to come up . . . if you have one installed. If you have Microsoft Office, then Outlook can function as a client, but I would recommend Agent or Xnews myself. If you don't want to worry about setting up a client, use Tile.Net to locate the newsgroup you want, then see if Google has it archived.

## MAILING LISTS

As previously mentioned, mailing lists are somewhat limited in usefulness when performing a modern job hunt, but your situation may be the exception. If so, try these:

### Topica

**http://lists.topica.com/dir/?cid=0**

On this website is a list of mailing lists for oodles of subjects; lots of newsletters are mixed in here, too. Not all of them are going to be useful, of course, but with a little work, you will know which ones are going to bear fruit as you are looking for contacts.

### Tile.Net

**http://tile.net/lists**

Here's Tile.Net again, with mailing lists organized by name, description, and domain; you will find Description most useful.

### L-Soft CataList

**www.lsoft.com/catalist.html**

Access to thousands (at last check: 53,924) of mailing lists, searchable by keyword, country of origin, and so forth.

## NETWORKING-SPECIFIC WEBSITES

I love invention and innovation. Much of the dot-com boom and bust happened (in my opinion) because would-be entrepreneurs didn't really innovate; they just tried to use the Internet as another avenue toward services that were already available offline. Very few Internet-based companies have been successful using this strategy.

The companies that *have* been successful on the Internet are the ones for which there is no offline equivalent; eBay is a perfect example. There wasn't a huge preexisting need or a problem crying loudly for solution, but eBay is arguably one of the most impressive of the Internet success stories. A solution before there is a problem: *that's* innovation.

I doubt that they can achieve the financial success of eBay, but the networking sites that have been created in the last few years are also excellent examples of innovation, for which there is no real offline equivalent (at least on this scale). In acknowledgment of the power of the networking concept, people are now using these intertwined networks of computers—the Internet—to increase the power of the real networks behind them: the people at those computers. And they are popular: other than the online dating sites (I kind of see these as the Internet's solution for the physical isolation it helps to create), the next most popular sites for connecting people are the business and job-hunting network sites.

This is not to say that the concept is perfect. There are many, many networking sites, and *not one of these sites is connected to any other*. The resulting networks are completely isolated.

Surveys show that people who register at these sites tend to visit often at first, but then their visits trail off, becoming more and more infrequent. It's okay at first, but who has the time to nurture hundreds of relationships?

My advice is to visit a bit, see which ones you like, and then register with one or two, *maybe* three at the most—certainly no more—and stick with those. At some point, even online, quality of relationships has to supercede quantity.

And although your immediate goal is to find a job, don't stop nurturing these relationships just because you've found employment. The people who helped *you* will, in turn, need *your* help one day. And you may find yourself job-hunting again in the not-so-distant future; no one will appreciate it if you only turn up on their virtual doorstep when *you* are in need.

Here is a sampling of ones most likely to be of use to you:

## LinkedIn

**www.linkedin.com**

LinkedIn is nothing less than an *excellent* business network site. In form, it is similar to others; in implementation, superior. When you sign up (registration is free), you enter your basic information—field, job title, geographic area, and so on—and indicate what kind of connections you are looking for and what kind of incoming contacts you are willing to accept. For example, if you currently own a business, you could indicate that you are open to inquiries about employment at your business, but naturally you don't want people sending you job offers for yourself.

You then go on to invite people to enter your network—you cannot draw people in unless they actively want to be included. As the people that you know join, and the people they know join, your network grows. At LinkedIn, your network is defined as a maximum of four levels, or degrees, out to a friend of a friend of a friend of a friend. For example, if only five people join at each level, that is still a network of 625 people. In reality, it is likely to be far more.

LinkedIn also allows you to contact people who are not in your network, if they have said they are willing to accept such contacts (and naturally, you may allow such contacts as well). As is increasingly common, the site also offers "premium" memberships (meaning, of course, that it's gonna cost you) at various levels that include other services.

More than fifty thousand of LinkedIn's registrants consider themselves job-hunters, even if their current employers do not. In light of this, the site has added a number of features for job-hunters, including links to many job boards. For example, LinkedIn has been integrated into the SimplyHired job search engine so that when a company name comes up, you can automatically see if anyone in your LinkedIn network works there.

## MySpace

**www.myspace.com**

Some might think it odd that I should list MySpace here, but this site is tremendously popular, particularly with the young, and getting more popular all the time. It is not specifically intended for business relationships per se, but it is all about relationships, who is who, and who knows who. The site has been extremely responsive to the needs of its members, and I think it likely that as time passes it will be used more and more for making contacts that lead toward the workplace.

MySpace also has a forum area, with headings that include career and business subjects.

## Tribe

**www.tribe.net**

Tribe is very similar to LinkedIn but takes a larger worldview. Why limit your network contacts to just business? What about if you needed to buy a used car—would you rather buy from a stranger or from a friend of a friend? If you were looking for a roommate, would you rather run a newspaper ad or find candidates among your network? If you needed a new dentist, whose recommendation would you trust?

This is what Tribe is about. As with other networking sites, you invite people to join, you have easy access out to four degrees, and so on. But at Tribe, your network—of course, here it is called your *tribe*—can be used for many purposes. Job-hunting is, of course, included, and the site even has job postings. But you can also use your tribe for buying and selling, housing, recommendations, special interests, and so on. There are even messaging forums for common-interest discussions among registrants.

Tribe, and its many uses, does bring up an important point: this is all about *trust*. When you are inviting people to join your tribe, you should invite only the people you know well and trust. If a friend that you invited into your tribe sells another friend a used car with a blown engine, it's going to come back on you. The people you invite in are counting on your recommendation that all of the people you have invited to join are trustworthy, and so it goes, out through all *your* degrees and into *other* people's. Don't invite your sister's no-good kid, just to pad the numbers.

And of course this applies to all of the networking sites. When you invite someone into your network, you are inviting them into not just your network but also the networks of the hundreds and thousands of people who connect to you. These people are all—*every one of them*—depending on *your* judgment about those you have invited, just as you are depending on theirs. The system collapses if the people involved are not truthful, reliable, consistent, and principled.

## Ryze

**www.ryze.com**

Ryze is very similar to LinkedIn, with a bit of Tribe thrown in. It is not as popular as LinkedIn, and because the networks these websites encourage are all isolated from each other, that might be a problem.

## Corporate Alumni

**www.corporatealumni.com**

This site is intended for people who used to work together at various companies. The site encourages both ex-employees of a company, and the companies themselves, to create community areas on the site. Companies are encouraged to treat their ex-employees not as ex-employees, but as alumni—people once bonded by the common experience of working for that company. So the site would have areas for people who used to work at Lotus, Microsoft, Enron—well, maybe not Enron . . .

I think that as ideas go, this is a good one. As websites go, it is not. In my tests, many large companies that should have alumni areas by now didn't, and I kept encountering page errors throughout the site. But I am listing the site anyway, in the hope that it will soon fix itself and become the useful resource it was no doubt intended to be.

## The Career Mole

**www.thecareermole.com/index.php**

This site is built around a very interesting concept. When you are researching various companies, you would probably like to be able to talk to people that already work there, get a sense of what the company is like, and see if you would fit in. At the same time, many companies have a hard time finding reliable people and encourage their current employees to keep an eye out for new job candidates. Often, employees are given incentives or bonuses if they refer someone who is eventually hired.

Career Mole is a website designed for these people to meet each other. Employees at various companies can register there; persons looking for a job at that company can then get in touch and discuss the possibility of that employee sponsoring them through the application and interview process. Likewise, job-hunters can register at the site, and people who are currently working at companies in need of good people can scan those profiles and see if there are any that fit the company's current needs.

The website was started by some consultants from the investment banking industry, and of course it's easy to see how this idea would work better for some industries than others; likewise, I think the idea is better suited to the executive level than to others. But ideas such as this often take on a life of their own and go places their inventors never dreamed of. It will be interesting to keep an eye on Career Mole in the coming years.

## Classmates.com

**www.classmates.com**

Well, the site's marketing campaign is kind of pushy, but there are many people registered here; you may find it valuable to be one of them. They also focus on registering "alumni" from the military and past workplaces.

## Schoolnews.com

**www.schoolnews.com**

The goal of the site is to be a directory of the graduates from over thirty thousand high schools in the United States and Canada. Graduates must sign in to their database; they are not automatically added from registration rolls.

## Networking for Professionals (Possible $$ )

**www.networkingforprofessionals.com**

Networking for Professionals is a little bit different from the standard networking model. You don't "invite" people you already know to help you form a network; NFP is a site for when you want to meet people that you don't already know, people that your network might not otherwise lead you to. All who sign up are here to meet people they otherwise would probably *not* find.

When you sign up, you enter your personal information and can post a resume; then you indicate what sort of business relationships you are interested in cultivating. You can also search the database of members to find professionals in certain fields.

Their membership fees and offers change over time; as I write, some people may join for free if they meet certain criteria, so if the site interests you, check and see if you qualify.

## Tools for Networking on the Internet

**www.quintcareers.com/Internet_networking_sources.html#online_communities**

An excellent list of various networking resources available on the Internet.

## Social Networking Services Meta List

**http://socialsoftware.weblogsinc.com/2005/02/14/home-of-the-social-networking-services-meta-list/**

Here you will find lists of hundreds of networking sites: business networking, common interest networking, dating, meeting facilitation sites. Very extensive.

## AN ONLINE COMMUNITY

When talking about networking and communities, we have to look at the one website that best reflects the places where we live:

**www.craigslist.org**

Craigslist describes itself as an "online community"; it's a good description. Originally started in the San Francisco Bay Area, craigslist has quickly grown into a series of websites all over the world. The site is nothing special to look at, but the minimalist approach fits it well; craigslist is about function and getting the job done. Style is not the point. Instead, you come here to look for a job, sell your dishwasher or buy a car, find out where to catch some live music this weekend, join in discussion groups on a variety of subjects, find an apartment or meet that special person, register to vote—in short, it is an online reflection of the places where we live—a community.

More particularly, and somewhat redundantly, there is the "community" section (the site, you'll notice, doesn't really believe in uppercase titles), which is a series of running forums on different subjects. You can use this community section to connect with people in the same line of work, start a job club, look for investors for your new business, and so on; almost anything goes.

As time passes, craigslist is becoming more popular as a place for employers to place job postings, in direct competition with sites like Monster and CareerBuilder—craigslist charges far less, and it has the advantage of being more focused on the local community (for example, Los Angeles job hunters don't have to weed out Boston job postings). Another section allows you to post, and look for, "gigs," which are typically one-day (or less) jobs. If you are still job-hunting when the savings run out and need to pick up some short-term work—as well as look for something more permanent *and* make connections with people who can help—then craigslist is the place to go.

## ANOTHER KIND OF NETWORKING: THE JOB CLUB

Here's an interesting little tidbit: one of the most successful ways of finding a job is by picking up the phone book, calling around to the businesses listed in the fields you are interested in, and asking if they have any job openings. Studies show that this method of job-hunting has a 69-percent success rate (meaning that out of a hundred people who use *only* this method in their job hunt, sixty-nine of them will be successful). Now, here is the interesting part: if you do *exactly* the same thing, but you do it as part of a group of people who are all job-hunting this way, the rate of success jumps to 84 percent.

The primary reason for this higher success rate is that the people in the group talk, and they tell each other what they each have found. You may not have had any luck today, but you talked to a guy who happened to mention that he is looking for someone in the same line of work as Bob, who is sitting over there near the end of the table. And of course, Bob doesn't have anything that can help you right now, but sitting across from Bob is Mary, and Mary just talked to a guy who knows a couple of companies that might be interested in someone like you, and so on. Had these people in the group *not* been talking with each other, their likelihood of job hunting success would be the same as if they each had been doing it alone.

There are job clubs and similar organizations all over the country. Most are free; often they will have guest speakers and other resources that can help you greatly in your job hunt. And every other person in the room is usually happy to help you. How often does that happen?

Job-Hunt—Networking Resources by State

**www.job-hunt.org/job-search-networking/job-search-networking.shtml**

One of the best pages on Susan Joyce's most excellent site. Choose the state you are interested in, and you will find links to job clubs and other resources, both for networking and for job-hunting in general.

## ANONYMOUS NETWORKING

Well, it's not really networking in the usual sense; it's more like peeking over others' shoulders to see what they are up to. For instance, there are sites on the Internet where people share their favorite websites, dealing with myriad subjects. Sometimes the subject is job-hunting; a quick search of the site will reveal if anything useful to your job hunt has been posted lately. Try these two, for example:

### del.icio.us

**http://del.icio.us**

A database of websites and the tags (one-word descriptions) associated with them.

### furl

**www.furl.net**

Sharing favorites (bookmarks) with others is not furl's primary goal, but is one of the things that can be done here. A companion site of LookSmart.

## NETWORKING WITH BLOGS

Using blogs as a job-hunting resource is discussed more thoroughly in the next chapter. For now, though, you may want to consider starting your own. If you have a certain amount of knowledge, experience, and authority in your field, blogging can help you share that with others as well as being a way of forming a body of visible work to which you can point prospective employers. Moreover, your blog may serve to draw other people to you who are interested in your writings; these people may, in turn, help you in your job hunt. Much of the job hunt is the process of making yourself visible to employers; blogging is one approach to doing that. You can start a blog at no charge by going to **www.blogger.com**.

## EMAIL

I cannot talk about contacts on the Internet without discussing the main method of communication on the Internet. How well—or how badly—you use email can have a significant effect on your ability to bring your job hunt to a successful conclusion.

From the employer's point of view, job-hunting is not so much a process of *selection* as it is a process of *elimination*. *This* person has spelling errors on his resume, *this* person never finished his degree, *this* person hasn't returned my calls . . . from the employer's point of view, the pile of applications or resumes gets thinner and more manageable.

When you are job-hunting online, the primary impression that people have of you is from your emails to them. If you dash off quick notes with sentence fragments, spelling errors, and poor grammar, you may never get to make an impression on them in person. Use email as a way of getting your communication to a person quickly, but don't let that sense of speed and efficiency slop over into the way you write. Email's main drawback as a communication method is that it lacks tone. Humor, irony, and other more subtle aspects of communication do not always work well in emails. When job-hunting, leave such shadings out of your email communications.

Note that prospective employers, people you would like to add to your network—in fact, *anyone* you want to make a good impression on during your job hunt, may not get the impression of you that you want if you have an email name like "sexykitten2" or "12pack-bob." Your ISP will usually rent you extra email addresses for dirt cheap. You don't have to get rid of your current fun-sounding email address; just get an additional one for your job hunt, with a name that sounds more businesslike.

Additionally, when using email:

- Take the time to learn how to use at least the basic features of your email client: do you know how to send and receive email attachments, use the address book, set the spam filters? You should learn how to use these features *before* you need to.

- Set your email program to send messages as plain text; don't send emails with HTML formatting, fancy fonts, or colored text. The person receiving your email may not be using the same email program as you, may not have the same features, or may have their options set differently. As a consequence, your emails may look like gibberish when received. If you must send formatted text, send it as an attachment to an email, using a standard word processing program like Microsoft Word (though don't send email attachments unless they are requested). Always explain in the body of the email what the attachment is.

- Make sure the subject line is short, pithy, and accurate. It doesn't hurt to repeat the subject line as a "Re:" at the top of the email text.

## SECURITY AND SPAM

During the course of your job hunt, you will be exchanging emails with many people you don't know well, or at all. Email is more likely to infect you with a computer virus than anything else you'll do with your computer during your job hunt, and accidentally infecting someone else could affect your chance of receiving a job offer from that person. So remember the standard warnings:

- *Never* respond to an unsolicited commercial pitch; don't even "opt out" from a mailing list you didn't ask to be on. Usually, this will only confirm your email address as a good one.

- *Never* give out passwords, credit card numbers, and so on, in response to what may look like a legitimate message from your bank, credit card company, ISP, eBay, PayPal, and so on. They will *never* ask you to do this; anyone that does is a crook masquerading as your bank or other service, hoping to get your passwords and credit card numbers.

- *Never* even click on a link in an unsolicited email (this can infect you with a virus, or automatically load a program onto your computer that spies on you).

- *Never* click on or open a program sent to you by email that you didn't ask for. Again, this can plant spyware on your computer that records your keystrokes and sends them to a hacker so he can cull out passwords and personal data.

- *Never* open a "security software patch" or anything similar, sent in an unsolicited email from what appears to be Microsoft or another software company. Don't even click on a *link*, even if it appears to indicate that it's at Microsoft or another legitimate company; it's not. Again, this is a spy program.

I personally use Eudora and Firefox—which are not Microsoft programs—when I am on the Internet. This is partly from long-standing habit and partly for security reasons. Because most people use Microsoft programs, those are the programs that hackers target when they are exploiting software security weaknesses (and all programs have such defects, regardless of manufacturer). No matter what programs you choose to use, make sure that you have antivirus software installed, active, and current.

These days spam—unwanted email advertisements—is just a fact of internet life we have to accept. The Can-Spam Act is a joke, and until the government actually comes up with a solution (I personally favor a tenth-of-a-cent fee for every email sent), we can only take steps to try and limit the flow.

Spammers have crawler programs, much like search engines do, that prowl the Internet looking for email addresses. Most of the addresses the crawlers find are no good, while a few are, and there's no way for the spammer to know which is which. Until, that is, you click on that "opt-out" link at the bottom of the email and tell the spammer your email address. Ah, now he knows he's got a good one.

And it doesn't matter that the spammer has to send out ten thousand emails to get one sale, or even a bite. Most of the offers are bogus, anyway; he just wants your credit card number and has no intention of delivering goods for payment.

Most of the current solutions to spam are problematic for the job-hunter. Some spam-blocking programs won't let you accept emails that aren't from people in your address book, but because you'll be getting lots of emails from people you don't know while you are networking and job-hunting, using such a program won't work. Other programs send the email back to the sender and make the person send it again. How's *that* for annoying? Forget that one.

No, as things are right now, the best you can do is just set the filters in your email client to catch surefire spammer words (most of which I cannot list here in a family book) and minimize the chances of their getting your email address in the first place. This means not posting your email address where the crawlers are most likely to find it, like on Usenet and message boards.

And if you *do* have to post your email in these places for some reason, try this: if your address is tomsmith@hotmail.com, you can type it as "tomsmith-at-hotmail.com." Most people will know to replace the "-at-" part with the "@" sign, but most spam crawlers will cruise right past it. (If you think the people you are corresponding with are not that Internet-savvy, add instructions for them to include the "@" sign.)

Here are a few links to help you use email more effectively:

### Harness Email

**www.learnthenet.com/english/section/email.html**

All about email.

### Email Netiquette

**www.library.yale.edu/training/netiquette**

From Yale University; short but very good. A must-read for every job-hunter.

### Email Etiquette

**www.emailreplies.com/#15formatting**

Though written as a set of rules for formulating email replies to customers, most of it applies to all email communications.

### Avoiding Spam

**http://cexx.org/spam.htm**

The best site I have seen on the subject. Another must-read.

### A Beginner's Guide to Effective Email

**www.webfoot.com/advice/email.top.html**

Though a bit dense for beginners, there are many good tips here for everybody, regardless of experience level.

### When Common Sense Fails

**www.freewarehof.org/email.html**

A humorous approach, no less valuable for that.

## THE MOST IMPORTANT PART OF YOUR JOB HUNT

The subject of email brings us to the most important thing you will do during your job-hunt: sending thank-you notes. A thank-you note is useless if it isn't prompt, so when someone does you a favor, email them a thank-you note within twenty-four hours. In addition, consider sending them *another* thank-you note by regular mail, through the U.S. Postal Service, as soon as possible. You wouldn't believe how many people have written to say that a simple thank-you note was what made the difference in their job hunt.

# 5. COUNSELING AND TESTING

**At this point,** if you have been using some of the less-effective job-hunting methods without success, you're probably feeling a bit lost and discouraged. Are you going about this the right way? Perhaps this would be a good time for more reading, some advice, maybe even a little career counseling.

Moreover, if you are using the most effective job-hunting method, as outlined in *What Color Is Your Parachute?*, then you must complete a thorough inventory of your skills, particularly the ones you most enjoy using. And of course you want to know: is advice and skills testing for the job-hunter available online?

Yes and no: the Internet can help you with some advice in your job hunt, but it cannot replace a live, face-to-face career counselor. It can help you with some basic skills tests, but the exercises in *Parachute* are more in-depth and enlightening than any tests you will find online. Because the simple fact is this: as hard as it is for most people to understand computers, it's a lot harder for computers to understand people.

In fact, the experts have been arguing for years about the effectiveness of *any* assessment tool when it comes to accurately looking inside of people. We are amazingly complex beings, and any test we take will yield different answers on different days, depending on mood, energy level, recent experiences, how hungry we feel . . . Even professionals with years of training under their belt get it wrong a lot of the time. Given that, how is some ten-minute computer test going to divine our inner workings?

But that doesn't mean that these tests are always completely useless, either. Go ahead and avail yourself of what the Internet has to offer, as long as you realize that the best these instruments can do is give you some hints, suggestions, maybe a general direction that you can then explore to see if something is actually there. Do *not* let any of these tests make you run off in a new direction, crying *Eureka!* all the way. And if you become convinced that you *must* take some of the online tests that cost money, just remember that paying for the results does more for the tester's bank account than for the test's accuracy.

## ONLINE TESTS: PERSONALITY/TRAITS

Interactive online tests fall into two categories: personality tests and career or vocational tests, though sometimes the line between them gets a bit hazy. The majority of the personality tests/games/instruments online will yield results that indicate your personality "type." Clearly this is not the same as a career test, but as *Chicago Tribune* columnist Carol Kleiman once pointed out, it is important that your future job or career fit your personality, so personality is not without career *implications*, at the very least.

In my view, though, the fundamental defect of personality-type instruments is that they are great at illuminating the *style* with which you do any job, but they are often misguided at predicting which career(s) that implies. I can tell you from many years of experience: jobs and careers are defined by much more than type or style. Therefore, take all personality-type career suggestions with a huge grain of salt. On the other hand, they can stimulate your own ideas, which is always a good thing.

Some of these instruments, particularly the Myers-Briggs Type Indicator (MBTI), are much loved by many career counselors. Note that the actual Myers-Briggs Type Indicator is not offered for free on the Internet. But other tests, quizzes, or sorters dealing with personality type are, including those on the sites that follow.

## The Keirsey Temperament Sorter

**www.keirsey.com**

Author David Keirsey categorizes people by temperament, and it is possible that through a more complete understanding of your temperament you may find more insight into the type of work that is best for you.

This somewhat complex website has lengthy descriptions of the various temperaments, as well as links to the Keirsey Temperament Sorter, which is available in several languages besides English, ranging from Spanish and German to Japanese and Ukrainian. The site is interactive, and once you've answered its questions, it gives you its results in Myers-Briggs-Personality-Type language ("You are an ENFP")—with colored graphs. As I said, it is a rather complex site, and you will need to spend a little time here to fully understand what the test is telling you, but stick with it if you think it worthwhile.

## The Enneagram Institute

**www.enneagraminstitute.com/Tests_Battery.asp**

The Riso-Hudson Enneagram Type Indicator (RHETI) is another personality test, with the results grouping you among nine basic personality types. Though popular as personality tests go, how much it has to say about career choice is debatable. But the Enneagram, like other tests of this sort, may have career implications, and it's useful for stimulating self-awareness, self-observation, and growth.

This is the "official" Enneagram site; any other websites with the test will be licensing it from this site, so it has some authority (well . . . at least to the degree that you feel the Enneagram *has* authority). The URL indicated has a couple of versions of the Enneagram test (and others), ranging from free sample tests to the full Enneagram test, which takes forty minutes and costs $10.

## The RHETI Test

**www.9types.com/homepage.actual.html**
**www.9types.com/rheti/homepage.actual.html**

Another Enneagram site. The first URL is the site's home page, which has some explanation of the nine types, a link to another version of the RHETI test available on the site, plus links to other Enneagram and personality-type pages. The actual test is found at the second URL listed; it is a "sample" Enneagram test in that it has 38 of the usual 144 questions found on the full RHETI.

### The Enneagram: an Adventure in Self-Discovery

**www.ennea.com**

For those who want to do further research into the whole idea of the Enneagram, here you will find a very complete list of Enneagram resources, seminars, history, and so on. You will notice that the site is a member of the Enneagram WebRing. WebRings are virtual circles of like-minded websites; you can successively click on Next, Previous, or Random links to get to the next site in the Ring.

### ColorQuiz

**http://colorquiz.com**

Why do people tend to buy the brands of sugar that have blue on the package? Why do so many institutions have pink walls? It has been shown that color has much to do with human personality and motivation. Based on the famous work of Dr. Max Luscher, this simple test is free, takes five minutes, and is different from most personality tests in that all you do is click on colors.

### The Classic IQ Test

**http://web.tickle.com/tests/uiq/authorize/register.jsp?url=/tests/uiq/index.jsp**

Probably the best free IQ test available on the Web; you may have seen it as you've clicked around, at a wide variety of sites linked to Tickle. You can take the test, and get your basic score, for free. More detailed results are available for a price (which is $12.95 currently), but you'll get signed up for a "subscription," an unfortunately common web marketing gimmick these days. (On the other hand, maybe the fact that you paid money is a kind of intelligence test in itself.)

### HumanMetrics: Jung Typology Test

**www.humanmetrics.com/cgi-win/JTypes1.htm**

A free test, based on the Myers-Briggs.

## ONLINE TESTS: CAREERS

We turn now from personality tests to career tests, also called vocational tests. Before you look at these, you should familiarize yourself with the Five (unless I think of more) Rules about Taking Online Career Tests.

1. No test can measure *you*; it can only describe the family to which you belong. Tests tend to divide the population into what we might call groups or tribes or families—namely, all those people who answered the test the same way you did. It all comes out as: "You are an ISFJ." Or "You are an SAE" or "You are a 'Blue.'" The results are an accurate description of that tribe, that family of people, in general, but they may or may not be true, in every respect, of *you*. So when you see your test results, keep in mind that these are the test results for the defined group that answered the questions the same way you did. As you can see by looking at the various tests, the number of groups and how they are defined can seem a bit arbitrary. You may be exactly like that group or you may be different in important ways.

2. Don't predetermine how you want the test to come out. Stay loose and open to new ideas. It's easy to have an emotional investment in the test coming out a certain way. Once, while taking a test about geographical preferences in the United States in which job-hunters had to prioritize a number of factors, one woman was long-delayed in arriving at an answer. When asked if she was running into any problems, she said, "No, I'm just prioritizing it. And . . . I'm gonna keep on prioritizing it, until it comes out *Texas*!"

3. You're looking for clues, hunches, or suggestions rather than for a definitive picture that tells you exactly what you should do with your life. "A light bulb going off over my head" is how some people describe what they got out of taking a test—at the most. If your goal in taking such a test, or series of tests, is that you're just looking for light bulbs, you will enjoy these tests much more.

4. Take several tests, not just one. One may send you horribly down the wrong path. Three different tests can offer a more balanced picture or a more balanced set of clues. An online test isn't likely to be as insightful as one administered by a qualified psychologist or counselor, who may see things that you don't.

5. *Please* don't try to force your favorite online tests on your friends. You may take a particular test, think it's the best thing since the invention of the wheel, and try to "sell" it to everyone you meet. Don't. Just because it worked well for you does not mean it will work well for them. If you ignore this, your friends will start running when they see you coming.

As a corollary to this, it might be fun to talk with your friends about the results of qualitative tests, but do not compare scores for quantitative tests; the IQ test is a classic example. One person's score will always be higher; it's not a situation that brings out the best human qualities.

That said, on to the tests:

## The Princeton Review Career Quiz

**www.princetonreview.com/cte/quiz/default.asp?menuID=0&careers=6**

A twenty-four-question quiz, related to the Birkman Method (which is a test, like the Meyers-Briggs, that is only available on the Internet for a fee). This one, however, is free and may have some good suggestions for you.

## Career Games

**www.careergames.com/fr-overview.html**

Here is one of the more useful (as well as fun) sites you will find during your job hunt. There are a number of self-assessment tools on the site, all in the form of one sort of game or another. Other job-hunting challenges—writing a resume, dealing with interview questions, salary negotiation—are presented as games as well. A really neat site, from job expert Daniel Porot.

## Dr. John L. Holland's Self-Directed Search 

**www.self-directed-search.com**

Over the years, John Holland's RIASEC system has proved to be extremely useful for assessment during the job search. The result of the test is a three-letter Holland Code, which you determine by taking his Self-Directed Search instrument. You can take the official test here and receive your results for $9.95. Though not officially sanctioned, there are similar tests available for free; see the following entries.

## The Career Interests Game

**http://career.missouri.edu/students/explore/thecareerinterestsgame.php**

This is a quick exercise, centered around Holland's RIASEC system, and based on the idea of someone walking into a room where a party is going on. The idea is that different groups (the various Holland RIASEC groups) are gathered in six separate areas of the room; you are attracted to people with interests similar to yours, so you join the various groups, thus revealing your Holland code. This simplified version of it, at the University of Missouri site, is called "The Career Interests Game," and though the exercise lacks the original central graphic, the site has otherwise done a good job of presenting it, with career links and so on. It gives you a good first guess at your three-letter Holland Code.

## The CareerKey Test

**www.careerkey.org/asp/your_personality/take_test.asp**

This test also provides you with your three-letter Holland Code.

## NY Career Zone

**www.nycareerzone.org/graphic/index.jsp**

This website, targeted primarily toward students in New York State, has a visually interesting version of Holland's RIASEC assessment. There is a related section of job titles for various fields.

## Holland Occupational Themes: Sample Self-Assessment

**www.soicc.state.nc.us/SOICC/planning/c1a.htm**

Another approach to finding your Holland Code.

## Career Briefs

**www.soicc.state.nc.us/SOICC/info/briefs.htm**

This is a listing of occupations and descriptions; the Holland Codes for each occupation are included, so if you have taken any of the tests here, or otherwise have some idea of your code, then some browsing through this site can give you some ideas for careers.

## HotJobs Career Tests

**http://hotjobs.careerid.com/articles.html**

The three basic tests here may give you some career guidance.

## CareerPlanner.com $$

**www.careerplanner.com**

CareerPlanner has a Holland-type test on this page; it will cost you from $19.95 to $29.95, depending on how fast you want your results back. If you click on the link that says, "If you decide not to buy right now, click here," you may be taken to its page at **www.careerplanner.com/Career-Test-Career-Search/Discount25.cfm**, which will give you a 25 percent discount. The discount may not be there by the time you try it, but on the other hand, it's been like this for four years, so it probably won't change real soon.

## Manifest Your Potential

**www.manifestyourpotential.com**

Kind of a quirky site, but there are a number of skills and interest tests as well as articles about achieving your potential.

## The Career Values Test

**www.stewartcoopercoon.com/jobsearch/career values/**

A quick way of identifying the things you value most in a career, from the mind of well-known job expert Dick Knowdell.

## JASPER

**http://my.monster.com/JobStrengthProfile/Intro.aspx**

This is a job assets and strengths profiler from Monster, which says it is "the new standard in career testing and assessment." Well, I don't know about *that*, but it is well designed and visually interesting. Too bad all websites aren't as engaging with their presentation.

## 43 Things

**www.43things.com**

If you are having problems identifying your interests and goals, or making contact with people who have interests similar to yours, try this website. The 43 Things site is where people go to list their goals and dreams. Maybe yours is the same as someone else's; maybe theirs will stimulate your thinking.

## ARTICLES AND ADVICE

Here is a selection of online articles with more about testing and advice:

### A Guide to Going Online for Self-Assessment Tools

**www.careerjournal.com/jobhunting/usingnet/20030429-dikel.html**

From the *Wall Street Journal* site, this is an article by jobs expert Margaret Dikel.

### Top Jobs Matching Your Interests and Needs

**www.princetonreview.com/cte/articles/plan/tenjobs.asp**

If you want some ideas for possible careers or jobs, you will find lists here like, "The Top Ten Jobs for People Who Can't Stand Ties or Pantyhose" or "The Top Ten Jobs for People Who Like to Work with Their Hands" . . . like that.

### Highest Paying Jobs

**www.resumagic.com/highestpayingjobs.html**

Lists of the jobs with the highest salaries (national averages, of course) for no college education and for two-year, four-year, and graduate degrees.

### The Best and the Worst

**www.careerjournal.com/jobhunting/change/20020507-lee.html**

In this brief article from the *Wall Street Journal* site, you'll find links to lists of the "ten best" and the "ten worst" jobs in America.

## TRANSFERABLE SKILLS

Readers of *What Color Is Your Parachute?* are familiar with the concept of transferable skills: essentially, that you are defined not by your job title, but by the skills that you possess, which are transferable from, and to, any occupation. It will come as no surprise to you that there are transferable skills tests available on the Internet:

### Transferable Skills Survey

**www.d.umn.edu/student/loon/car/self/career_transfer_survey.html**

From the University of Minnesota, a quick online test of your transferable skills. Test results will show you your strongest and weakest areas.

### Transferable Job Skills

**www.quintcareers.com/transferable_skills.html**

From Quintessential Careers, an article series that details the concept of transferable skills, with lists of skills and advice about how to emphasize these in your resumes and cover letters.

### Skills Search

**http://online.onetcenter.org/skills**

From O*Net OnLine, this quick test will help you link your skills to possible occupations, using the U.S. Department of Labor's database. Once you've identified these occupations, you can look at lots of current information about them, including salary level, hiring rates, and so on.

### Motivated Skills Test

**www.stewartcoopercoon.com/jobsearch/freejobsearchtests.phtml**

Some experts say that it is not your transferable skills that matter, but the ones you most enjoy using. They call these *motivated skills* or *key skills*. There is a test you can take on this site, to help you identify yours.

### Skills Analysis

**www.uwrf.edu/ccs/assets/documents/handouts/skills_analysis.pdf**

A good introduction to skills analysis from the University of Wisconsin website.

## EDUCATION

Maybe, after doing a lot of soul-searching, you have decided that you will never get the job or career you want without further education. Don't feel bad; there's a lot of that going around. On the next page you'll find some places to start.

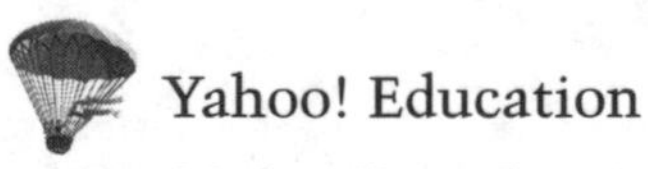

## Yahoo! Education

**http://education.yahoo.com**

I happen to think that this is the most useful page that Yahoo! has, and that's saying quite a bit. From here, you can search for specific schools, look for schools that offer certain courses or degrees, even find out what schools have online classes, enabling you, in many cases, to get your degree over the Internet. Also a good place to check out K–12 schools for the kids, although I prefer the sites listed in chapter 6 in the Work in Education section. Anyway, a terrific site.

## Academic Info

**www.academicinfo.net**

A great site for researching degree programs (online and offline), schools, test preparation . . . everything to do with education.

## Vocational and Technical Schools Directory

**www.votechdirect.com**

Online schools are included in the database as well.

## National Directory of Women's Education and Training Programs

**http://associationdigital.com/womenwork/online/directory/default.aspx**

This page gives you access to organizations that offer training and degree programs for women, listed by state. Often the accent is on displaced homemakers, working mothers, and women in transition.

## Google University Search

**www.google.com/options/universities.html**

This is a nice service, implemented strangely. From the extensive alphabetical list of universities, pick the one you want. That doesn't lead you to the school's web page; it brings you to a database, that Google has compiled, of what is on each university's web server. You then need to enter a search term—"courses," "schedule," or the like—to get information. (I entered "*.*" out of unconscious habit and got a browsable list of what was on the server.)

### U.S. News—eLearning Guide

**www.usnews.com/usnews/edu/elearning/elhome.htm**

This site contains a database of colleges and universities, public and private, that offer online education.

### College Planning Resources

**www.quintcareers.com/college_planning.html**

A list of resources for people who are planning to attend college, adults who need to return to school, and so on.

### Education Newsgroups

**www.careers.org/education/03-70-educational-newsgroups.html**

A list of newsgroups dedicated to education.

### Distance Learning

**www.careers.org/education/00-00-distance-learning.html**

A list of schools with online courses.

## FOR FURTHER HELP: CAREER COUNSELING OFFICES

If you still need more in the way of career counseling, you should take a look at all of the career offices on the Internet. There are essentially two kinds: career centers at colleges and universities and the various state government career offices. Though not traditionally renowned for their job-hunting acumen, many of the state employment development departments have improved mightily in the last few years. A few are surprisingly good.

### College Career Centers

**www.jobweb.com/article.aspx?id=648&linkidentifier=id&itemid=648**

From JobWeb, this is a list of career centers at colleges around the United States, as well as some in Canada, the United Kingdom, and Australia.

### Career Centers

**www.servicelocator.org**

From Career One Stop, this page provides access to a large number of career resource centers around the United States.

### State Government Job Resources

**www.careers.org/career-reference/06-64-state-government-job-resources.html**

Every state has resources for helping the job-hunter; this page, from the Careers.Org website, lists various resources available in each of the fifty states.

## BLOGS

Whenever someone asks me if I like a certain musician or actor or writer or film director, I always get this strange "yeah, but . . ." feeling. If I say I like them, doesn't that mean I am endorsing everything they have done? For example, Dustin Hoffman is a great actor, but remember *Ishtar*? Stephen Spielberg is one of our best directors . . . but I had the misfortune of seeing *Hook*. (And now that I think about it, Dustin was in *that* one, too.) The Beatles—wow, one of the best bands ever, but to my ears the *White Album* was a mess . . . like that.

Well, this is kind of how I feel about blogs. "Blog" is a contraction of "web log"; it's kind of a running commentary, most often written by a single person on a regular basis. Some are unfocused, meaning the blogger writes about whatever happened to fall out of the sky in the blogger's vicinity that day. Other blogs have a subject or theme. There are a few whose theme, in theory at least, is job-hunting.

As is true with most blogs, not everything the job-hunting bloggers have to say is helpful. In fact, sometimes you have to wade through an awful lot of chaff to find the grain. For the most part, any resources and advice they have to offer is available—or done better—elsewhere.

But exceptions exist. To find blogs about job-hunting, do a search on "career blog" or "job hunt blog" and see what comes up.

Blog sites archive their entries, which are searchable. Also, blog writers are usually happy to respond to concise emails. "Concise" is the operative word: you should keep any requests you have reasonable, and remember that although your life story *is* really fascinating, their time is limited.

### Secrets of the Job Hunt

**http://secretsofthejobhunt.blogspot.com**

Chris Russell's site is pretty good; he knows his subject and writes well.

### Get That Job!

**http://getthatjob.blogspot.com**

### CyberJournalist

**www.cyberjournalist.net/cyberjournalists.php**

At this site, you can find a list of blogs around the Web.

## ONE-ON-ONE CAREER COUNSELING

Your problem may be such that none of the resources I have listed, or that you have diligently searched for on your own, are able to help you. You may need the assistance of a professional. In this case, you are in luck:

### Email a Career Counselor for Free

**www.jobhuntersbible.com/counseling/sec_page.php?sub_item=148**

At the Job-Hunter's Bible site, there is a free service for people who have tried very hard to solve their job-hunt problems using *What Color Is Your Parachute?* but feel they are stuck. It is not the first place you should turn, but neither should you feel reticent about taking advantage of this unique resource. Go to this page for more information.

## OFFLINE CAREER COUNSELING

In the back of *What Color Is Your Parachute?* is an appendix with a list of professional career counselors, across the country and around the world, all of whom are familiar with the principles in the latest edition of *Parachute*. There's likely to be one near you, regardless of where you live. Some of the counselors listed are also willing to counsel through email or on the telephone.

The services of these professionals are not free, nor should you expect them to be. And you should not jump for a counselor as your first move. But as with any licensed professional, be it a doctor, lawyer, or career counselor, there are times when you need to call for expert help.

# 6. ONLINE RESEARCH

**Back in chapter 1,** I gave you a list of the various job hunting methods, numbered from least effective to the most effective, and I have used that list as a general way of organizing this book. We have looked at all of the methods that are statistically less effective; it is now time to look at the two most effective job-hunting methods on that list. They are:

8. Identify the firms in your area doing the kind of work you are good at and contact them to see if they need someone like you. The success rate is about 69 percent.

9. Do the kind of creative job hunt outlined in this book and described in great detail in *What Color Is Your Parachute?* This method has a success rate of 86 percent.

Let's look first at a brief overview of #9, which is commonly referred to as the Parachute process (for a more complete description, see the chart in *Parachute* on page 251, for the 2008 edition anyway; it will tend to move around a bit from year to year):

a. Identify your *transferable skills*. The skills that you possess are not confined to any single field or job title. They can be used anywhere and are transferable, hence the term. Furthermore, you must prioritize these skills so that you know which of your transferable skills are the ones you most enjoy using. (The latest buzzword is *motivated skills*, but don't worry, it'll change soon.)

   You can identify these skills using the exercises in *Parachute* and any useful online tests from chapter 5.

b. Identify the fields and industries you would like to work in. Are you drawn to health care? Do you like to work with your hands? Do you love the feel of wood? Do you really enjoy using computers? Do you hate being indoors? What makes time fly for you? When you combine these with your list of favorite transferable skills, you can start identifying possible job titles.

c. Once you have a job title or other useful description of the work you would like to do, you should research different fields and industries to see what companies (in your chosen geographic area) do the kind of work you are interested in.

d. Research these companies thoroughly. Identify the ones that have the kind of work environment you prefer and are most appealing to you.

e. From the resulting list of companies you have chosen, identify the person with the power to hire.

f. Cut no corners; take no shortcuts.

If you think about it, method #8 on the list is very similar to method #9, the Parachute process. It does lack the skills and fields identification in steps a and b, assuming that you have a job title or other job description and are ready to start identifying companies in your chosen area that do the kind of work you are interested in.

Note that when I say "job title" you should realize that I am really talking about a job description. You could describe a job as "a situation where, using my medical training, I work with doctors in a clinical or hospital setting, concentrating on direct patient care," or you could say, "I want to be a nurse." When you have identified the skills you want to use and the field in which you want to use them, you may or may not come up with a job title; if you don't, that doesn't mean that such a job doesn't exist or cannot be found. It only means that there isn't a short, handy description in common use yet. But not so many years ago, "systems analyst," "forensic DNA technician," or "network support specialist" (not to mention "internet job-hunting author") wouldn't have meant much to most people. Someone invented those job titles and the unique combination of skill sets and environments involved with them. The world is constantly changing, and the world of work changes with it. Don't let the lack of a job title stop you.

It doesn't matter which of these most-successful job-hunting methods you are using; 90 percent of the process is research. Not all of this is best done online—just like every other part of your job hunt, you will seriously handicap yourself if you *only* use the Internet. But when performing company and industry research, an amazing amount of data *is* available online, with more available every day.

This means that you are now reading what is probably the most important chapter in this book. When it comes to the most effective job-hunting methods, your ability to conduct meaningful research becomes absolutely essential. And as salary level rises, as the required experience and skill set of the applicant goes up, as the responsibility inherent in the prospective job increases, so does the amount of research required to identify such positions.

The research you are likely to perform during your job hunt falls into two broad types: basic online research and more specific job-hunting research. The first type is primarily an act of broad discovery, using tools and techniques that that are useful for many types of research, whether you are job-hunting or not. This kind of research uses search engines, directories, databases, and other internet resources to find many kinds of information, for many purposes. When performing this kind of research, you will often start off knowing almost nothing—sometimes you won't even know the right questions to ask!—but as you proceed, you will collect more and more information until things start to become clear. It is primarily a broadening and collecting process.

The second type of research involves researching industries, salaries, places to live, companies to work for, and so on. In many ways, it is a narrowing and focusing process, very much aimed at job-hunting in particular. General search tools are not as useful here, and the focus is more on business and job-hunting websites.

## INTERNET RESEARCH—THE BROAD TOOLS

Research is where the Internet truly excels. It is a worldwide library at your fingertips, which you can access anytime, day or night, without ever leaving your home—a researcher's dream. Of course, you must do your research with care and intelligence; there is so much available online that you can be easily overwhelmed, and too much information can be just as bad as no information.

To help with basic online research, special types of websites have been created, the primary purpose of which is to tell you where the data is. The two kinds of sites you will find most useful in this regard are directories and search engines.

## DIRECTORIES

Directories are places where you will find websites—from a few to thousands—organized by subject. Unlike search engines, which determine results by software, directories are organized mostly by human hand.

The saying goes, "browse to learn, search to find." Generally speaking, directories are for generating ideas, and search engines are for gathering specific data. Most directories are hierarchically organized by subject; you start with a general heading and move toward more specific groupings. Conversely, a search engine looks for data that will fit with certain keywords, regardless of subject; but you need to know the keywords to look for. So use directories when you need some ideas to help you narrow things down, or when you are looking at a subject's broader aspects.

Because directories are hierarchically organized by subject, they are often the best place to start when looking for online data. Even if you don't find exactly what you are looking for, the subject categories themselves can help you with ideas on what keywords to use when you move on to search engines.

You may notice that, because they are compiled by human hand, the entries in some directories are not as current as you might like;

others are meticulously updated. With directories, one size does not fit all. There is a lot of variation among different directories—just because it isn't in one does not mean that it isn't in another.

## Open Directory Project

**www.dmoz.org**

The largest directory on the Web, with over 4.8 million sites in close to 600,000 subject categories. As the name implies, this is an all-volunteer project. On the one hand, this gives the directory its large size, but it also means that some entries may not be as up-to-date as you might hope. Also, because each entry is examined and reviewed by a real person, and there are *lots* of these real persons involved, there may be some slight bias now and then on the part of the editors, who, for the most part, are not professionals. Still, this is the obvious place to start when you are looking for subject information. As an example of the site's depth, check out the Careers page at **www.dmoz.org/Business/Employment/Careers**.

## Librarians' Internet Index

**http://lii.org**

Probably the best on the Internet. Entries include the date that they were last looked at by one of the directory's staff, so you will know how recent their site descriptions are. Next to Yahoo!, probably the most-used directory online.

## Yahoo!

**http://dir.yahoo.com**

One of the best-known sites on the Internet, for many reasons, Yahoo! still has the best directory for a commercial site. Some entries are "sponsored," obviously, but they are clearly marked (and occasionally useful themselves). As you know, Yahoo! also has a search engine, and you can limit your searches to the Yahoo! directory.

As an example of the difference between commercial and noncommercial sites, compare the Careers page at Open Directory Project with the Career Counseling page at Yahoo! (**http://dir.yahoo.com/Business_and_Economy/Shopping_and_Services/Employment/Career_Counseling**).

### InfoMine

**http://infomine.ucr.edu**

The directories just listed are mostly general directories. There are many specialized directories on the Internet as well. How do we find these directories? Why, we look in a *directory* directory, of course.

InfoMine is halfway between a directory and a search engine. You tender a query, and InfoMine, rather than kicking back pertinent web pages, will return resources—databases, libraries, directory sites, and so forth—where you are likely to find the kind of information you are looking for. You can specify the types of resources you want to search; in many cases, you can also browse through the resource types.

### Internet Public Library

**www.ipl.org**

Another excellent directory. Not always a lot of depth here, but the entries tend to be current, authoritative, and worth checking out for your research.

Though not related directly to job-hunting, one of the areas of the IPL that I like best is the Reading Room, with links to books published on the Internet. Want to read the *Iliad*? Maybe an actual first edition of *Huckleberry Finn* with the original E. W. Kemble illustrations? How is this going to help your job hunt? I don't know; forget I mentioned it.

## SEARCH ENGINES

Constantly growing and changing, the Internet is like a library with no card index, no titles on the book spines, and no head librarian. At any given moment, no one knows everything that is there. Directories know only what a human has entered into them, and they certainly cannot keep up with the Internet's rapid rate of change. So when directories are insufficient, we need to turn to a different tool: the search engine.

There are many search engines on the Internet. Some are better than others for certain tasks—sometimes *much* better. To understand why, and to pick the best engine(s) for your research, we should look at how search engines do what they do.

It's a gross oversimplification, but a search engine is a bit like the Find command in your word processor. When you want to find a certain part of a document, you enter a keyword into the Find command, and the word-processor software looks for a match.

That's kind of the way search engines work. In their case, you could say that the Internet is the document—but it's actually more complex than that, and it is in this complexity that we find the differences between the many search engines available. The differences can be broken down into three factors:

- The way they index the Web
- The way they search the index, return results, and rank the results (by how closely the engine thinks they match your query—the "relevance")
- The way they deal with advertising and "sponsored matches"

These three factors affect the quality of the results that the search engine will return to you when you make a search query. Let's look at each more closely.

## The Way They Index the Web

Search engines are computer programs. They use a software tool called a "crawler" or "spider" to prowl the Internet and create a database of pointers to various web pages (millions of them). Then, when a researcher—you, for instance—comes along and says, "Find me data on subject X," the search engine kicks out those addresses from its indexed database that have information it thinks is relevant to your request.

Let me emphasize that: a search engine does *not* return data directly from the Web. It returns data from its *index* of the Web.

The methods used to index the Web can vary significantly from one search engine to another. This means that each search engine's data index can be very different, and that affects how each responds to your search queries.

## The Way They Search the Index

As I said, search engines do not search the Internet directly; they search the database they have compiled about the Internet. It is not unusual for different search engines to give their crawlers different instructions on what to look for on the Web. This means that their databases will be very different. In other cases, different engines use different technology to search similar databases. Both of these factors will cause different data to be returned in response to a search query. Nor are all search technologies, and the methods they use, equal in effectiveness. This means that some search engines are more effective at finding your data than others. So when you are conducting an information search, you should not necessarily depend on a single engine to give you all of the information that is available out there.

## The Way They Deal with Advertising and Sponsored Matches

All of the search engines are there to make money. Some will return, along with your search results (but clearly separate), a list of short ads from companies that offer products and services that are usually somewhat related to your search results, as a kind of targeted advertising. Another common practice is to include, in the list of results, websites that have paid to be placed there. Usually they will have at least *something* to do with your query . . . maybe. These are called "sponsored matches"; if you then click on one of these, the search engine gets paid. Generally, these results are clearly marked as sponsored. However, some search engines don't tell you which of the sites it is listing are sponsored, regardless of whether those sites rank high in relevance to your search query. This practice costs you time and corrupts your search results; in my mind, these search engines should be avoided.

## USING SEARCH ENGINES

One of the key differences among the various search engines is how they rank the data they have culled from the Web and prioritize it for your search query—you *did* want the most relevant results first, rather than buried here and there in a thousand pages of URLs, right? This is the secret sauce of the search engine field, and it is what determines how good your search results are and how happy you are with a particular search engine.

But part of the responsibility is yours. There is far more to using search engines effectively than just typing in the first words that come to mind. There are many ways to use keywords, Boolean terms, and specific search engine commands to help you use the search engines most effectively. To this end, I direct you to a few places where you can learn more about using search engines and their language:

### Web Searching Tutorial

**www.askscott.com/tindex.html**

This is one of the best tutorials on web search engines that I have found. Easy to understand, yet very complete.

### A Primer in Boolean Logic

**www.internettutorials.net/boolean.html**

When structuring search queries, it's helpful to understand how Boolean logic works, because this is how most search engines parse your requests. This explains how to structure your search queries for more effective results.

### University of South Carolina: Basic Search Tips

**www.sc.edu/beaufort/library/pages/bones/lesson7.shtml**

A quick intro on how to formulate search queries. There are links to finding more in-depth information, if you like.

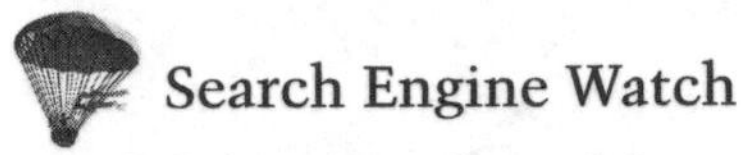

### Search Engine Watch

**http://searchenginewatch.com**

This site is all about search engines. Very current; this site, more than any other, keeps its finger on the pulse of the search engine industry (and, yes, it is an industry; the aggregate profits are huge). You can find tips for using search engines, as well as information on specific engines—who uses whose database, who just bought up whom, what new features are being offered at a particular search site . . . like that.

Also, every search engine has its own little quirks and special features. Be sure to visit the help pages of the engine you are using.

## BEST SEARCH ENGINES

Some search engines are better at finding certain types of data. I'll start with the general search engines and the ones I believe to be best:

### Google

**www.google.com**

In the time since this book was first published, Google has come to dominate the search engine arena on the Web, mainly because it does what it does better than the others. It is faster, the results it offers are more likely to be relevant to your request, and it doesn't hide commercial results in relevant data. It also has indexed approximately eight million web pages, which is roughly twice as much as any other search engine. You may have your own favorite search engine that you prefer to use instead. As you wish; but realize that no other search engine comes close to Google's wide reach and immense resources. If you choose not to use it, you should have very clear reasons.

When using Google, you may target different parts of the Web, using Google's collection of web pages, images, news, and so on. But there's a lot more to Google. For example, Google has a directory, similar to Yahoo!'s, at **www.google.com/dirhp**. You can also do full patent searches, and the company is in the process of creating a huge database of books, both current and classic.

Google is constantly experimenting with new data services. At Google Scholar, you can read many scientific papers—abstracts and full text—from publications around the world. So if you wanted to read, say, about the

"Effects of JC Virus Infection on Anti-Apoptotic Protein Surviving in Progressive Multifocal Leukoencephalopathy" (who wouldn't?), now you know where to go.

In addition, Google is always working on advanced ideas; some of these work out; others don't. Want to see where the different taxi cabs are located, right this minute, in your neighborhood, so you know which cab company to call for a ride? Want some free software to help you design web pages? Want to use your mobile phone to see who has the lowest price on certain products in your area? For these and other cool ideas that Google currently has in the works, go to **http://labs.google.com**.

For all of the features and abilities Google already gives you, it clearly deserves its reputation as *the* search engine for the Web.

### Yahoo! Search

**http://search.yahoo.com**

It seems like Yahoo! has been around as long as the Internet itself. At one time king of the web search hill, it has been largely overshadowed by Google. In some ways, that's a shame; Yahoo! still has much to offer. In particular, Yahoo! has always been a better directory than a search engine, and this remains true today—Yahoo!'s directory is second to none. Although it's plain to see how much influence Google continues to exert on Yahoo!, the underlying technologies are not identical, so don't neglect Yahoo! when searching and researching.

## CLUSTERING

How does a search engine decide what gets put at the top of the list of search results? One of the approaches for ranking search engine results involves page linking: how many other web pages link to this one? The theory goes that if a lot of other sites are linking to a certain web page, then they must like the data on that page. It's another way of saying that the data there has the ring of authority. Of course, the converse may also be true: if no one links to it, maybe the online community doesn't think the data there is so great. It isn't the only method used for ranking results, but with many search engines, it is the primary factor affecting what is at the top (and what isn't) when a search engine returns the results of a query.

But this technique has weaknesses. Relevance can artificially change due to bursts of interest from the online community (or fail to respond to interest that came after the page was ranked). Additionally, linking itself can be manipulated, a practice known as "Google bombing." It doesn't take too many web page operators to skew the ranking of the data that a search engine returns.

The first example of Google bombing I know of came soon after the U.S. invasion of Iraq. A Google search for "weapons of mass destruction" would bring up a very realistic-looking Google-style error page, saying that no such weapons could be found (you can view it at **www.coxar.pwp.blueyonder.co.uk**). Following that, some people got together and caused the query phrase "miserable failure," when typed into the major search engines, to return President Bush's biography from the White House website. And of course Bush supporters then Google bombed Hillary Clinton, Michael Moore, and others. You can read more about Google bombing at **http://en.wikipedia.org/wiki/Google_bomb** and **http://news.bbc.co.uk/2/hi/americas/3298443.stm**.

This would be just an interesting anecdote if it didn't reveal the flaws inherent in this type of relevance ranking, whether done purposefully or not. But how else can data be organized in search engine returns?

One interesting—and helpful—approach is *clustering*. Some search engines, rather than returning results in strict hierarchical order, cluster the results under various headings. For example, a search on "tension" might bring results grouped under headings for politics, headaches, musical instrument strings, physics, and so on. When results are returned this way, it is harder to make any single site artificially jump out at you—and of course, it is often a better way to zero in on the data that you want.

Here are a few search engines that use clustering:

## Ask

**www.ask.com**

The latest incarnation of Ask Jeeves, Ask is now a mature search engine, as well as a leader in using clustering technology to rank information in search returns.

### Clusty

**http://clusty.com**

Clusty is a search engine that returns its results in clusters; you can even have your results displayed in tag clouds. (Tag clouds rank subjects in a visually intuitive manner; you've probably seen them without knowing what you were looking at. See the explanation later in this chapter.) The actual search technology is from Vivisimo, so it tends to return results that are different in content from search engines like Google. Note also that Clusty partners with the job search engine Indeed.

### Mooter

**www.mooter.com**

Mooter's clusters are presented as a graphical formation resembling the spokes of a wheel. You can choose one of the spokes, where the clusters are broken down even further—it's pretty interesting. I was a bit disappointed that Mooter seems to return more sponsored results than most of the clustering-type search engines.

## METASEARCH TOOLS

In metasearch engines, your query is submitted to a number of search engines, then a few of the returns from each are combined into a list of results. In practical terms, you sacrifice depth for breadth—but that's not always a bad thing. If you want to get a quick overview of what's available for a certain search phrase, then a metasearch engine may be a good idea.

### Dogpile

**www.dogpile.com**

Dogpile is one of the better metasearchers. When searching, it uses Google, Yahoo!, Search, Ask, Live Search, About, MIVA, LookSmart, the Open Directory, and more. There are other engines and databases it uses to return a certain number of commercial results. The site has some nice features: it remembers your last few searches and suggests ways to refine your search. Because of the lack of depth, I believe that metasearchers are of limited use—kind of between a directory and a normal search engine—but Dogpile is one of the best in the bunch.

### Beaucoup!

**www.beaucoup.com**

A little different from your basic metasearch engine, Beaucoup! queries and returns results from Google, Yahoo!, AltaVista, Fast, Ask Jeeves, Lycos, MSN, WiseNut, HotBot, and AOL Search, and tells you from which each of its results came. You can also tell it to search only one of the engines at a time. However, because the metasearch engines don't return all the results you would get directly from, say, Google, you should just go to the source rather than use Beaucoup! this way. Sponsored results are clearly marked in a separate list from the relevant results.

In addition to the search engines listed here, Beaucoup! has other resources it can tap. There are some databases that you can direct the Beaucoup! search engine toward.

You may not find a lot of depth here, but what you will find—heck, it's what metasearch engines are *supposed* to do—is a tool that cuts broadly but not deeply. Once you start here, you can choose how to narrow your information hunt.

### KartOO

**www.kartoo.com**

KartOO is a metasearch engine that presents its results in visually appealing cluster maps. It's a very interesting site. When doing searches, it's not the first place to go, but its approach is so different that it not only may help you find different data than other engines, but it may also give you new ideas about how to conduct your search.

## SPECIALIZED SEARCH ENGINES

The search engines that I have recommended so far are all generalized search engines with large databases. However, there are a *lot* of smaller, specialized search engines out there. Remember, it is not the *technology* that characterizes the various search engines so much as their *databases*. It follows, then, that for a specialized search you don't need specialized technology as much as you need a specialized database. The following sites will help you find specialized search engines:

### A Collection of Special Search Engines

**www.leidenuniv.nl/ub/biv/specials.htm#Par62**

A very good list of special search engines and searchable directories. I am continually amazed at the riches on this site.

### All Search Engines

**www.allsearchengines.com**

The name is actually a bit misleading. In my time on this site, I have found it to be more of a subject directory than a search engine list, but there are hundreds of specialized search engines here as well. From a list of all U.S. government web servers, to hundreds of career sites—there is a *HUGE* amount of stuff here. I particularly like the page of public libraries online, listed at **www.allsearchengines.com/libraries.html**, and the list of foreign search engines, grouped by country, at **www.allsearchengines.com/foreign.html**.

### SearchEngines.com

**www.searchengines.com**

Not a search engine in itself, but a way to find the specialized search engines—kind of a search engine for search engines. The search engines on the site are organized in many ways, and you can find engines that are specific to certain countries or continents, ones that specialize in certain subject areas, and so on.

## BEYOND SEARCH ENGINES

Surprisingly, much of the Internet is beyond the reach of search engines; experts estimate that search engines give you access to only one-tenth to one-half of what is available online. The rest is hidden unless you know where to look for it.

To access this huge amount of data that search engines will not find for you, it is helpful to know why search engines are so limited in their reach. Much of it is too technical to list here, but there are three basic reasons:

- The search engines are told by their masters not to go to certain areas. For example, there are large databases on the Internet

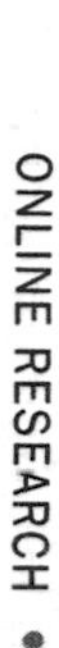

that are not profitable to index, or their data is in a form that is difficult for the search engines to digest.

- The search engines are told by the owners of the data to keep out. Not everyone wants to have their data indexed and available through Google or Yahoo! if it would, for instance, reduce their own profits to do so. There are commands that can be embedded in web pages that tell the search bots to keep out.

- The search engines are not smart enough to find the data, or perhaps they cannot even find the website that stores the data. If nobody is linking to a certain website yet, the crawler may not even be able to find the site.

And yet, much of this data might be helpful to you in your job hunt. Where is it, and how do you find it?

## DATABASES

There is a huge amount of information available in databases on the Web. Once you find them, their information is usually easily accessible. Most have a human-oriented interface that allows you to find the data they contain.

But the real problem is, how do you find the databases? Try these techniques:

- Add the word *database* or *archive* to your search engine inquiry. (An example might be "professional association AND database.") Even when the search engines haven't mined the information they contain, the engines usually know where the databases themselves are located.

- URL mining. When you find a URL with a question mark in it, erase everything in the URL from just before the question mark to the end, then press Enter. Occasionally you will turn up a database, or a link to one.

- Other sites on the Internet often know where good databases are and link to them—but rarely to just one. When you find a database, put the "link" command before its address, and plug that into a search engine. Although syntax varies from one engine to another, it will usually be something like the word "link," followed by a colon and then the site address you are curious about. For example, to see the sites that link to the Job Hunter's Bible website, using Google, you would type:

  **link:http://www.jobhuntersbible.com**

  Once you have the web addresses of all the sites that the search engine knows have links to the site you are interested in, you can go to those places and see where else *those* sites link to.

- Use the subject directories listed earlier, like the Librarians' Internet Index, the Open Directory Project, and so on. These will often point you to databases you can access.

## ANOTHER APPROACH TO FINDING DATA

Your time is limited, and there is far too much on the Internet for you to ever know all that is available. So it makes sense to use the experience of other people to find websites that might be useful:

### Del.icio.us

**http://del.icio.us/**

Suppose that every time you ran into a new website, you gave it a one-word description—we'll call it a "tag"—that describes the essence of that site, at least as you see it. Suppose *everyone* did the same thing. It wouldn't be unusual for different people to use the same word to describe the site, but on the other hand, it's also likely that many people would not use the same word; they see the site differently than you do. Over time, the tags associated with a website would form a pretty fair description of the site, and what is available there.

The next step would be having the ability to search these tags that have been associated with these websites. This would give you a whole new approach (very different from using search engines) to finding data on the Internet.

What I have just described is one way of looking at a website called Del.icio.us. Basically, it is a database of websites and the tags associated with them. Plug a term (or a series of terms joined by "+" signs) into the search box, and you'll get back a list of websites whose tags match your search terms. Sometimes the results are absolutely useless, and other times they are extremely useful and enlightening.

And speaking of tags, go to the page at **http://del.icio.us/tag/**; what this page shows is a "tag cloud." A tag cloud is a series of tags in which the words used most often to describe a site are in larger and bolder print than the words used less often. It's actually a very intuitive way of describing websites—and many other things. Some search engines use tag clouds to return results; Clusty (listed earlier, under clustering search engines) is one, and there is currently a wonderful search engine in beta form called Quintura (at **www.quintura.com**) that returns results in tag clouds. (Notice what happens when you place your mouse cursor on one of the tags in the cloud that Quintura returns.) Like many right-brain, intuitive approaches, tag clouds don't work for everyone. But when they do, it often allows that "quantum leap" or "Eureka" moment that we all wish we could call up on command . . . and never can.

## THE UNDERWEB

The part of the Internet that is beyond the reach of search engines is variously called the UnderWeb, the Invisible Web, the Deep Web, and similar names. Here are some other places to look for data on the UnderWeb:

### LibDex

**www.libdex.com**

This is an index to eighteen thousand libraries, many of which have online materials and databases that you can access.

## Resources and Databases—Purdue University Library

**www.lib.purdue.edu/eresources/**

Wow. An excellent page that directs you straight to many UnderWeb databases, grouped by subject. Also, take a look around the whole site while you are here; the library has a strong web presence, with current information and many special features.

## Educator's Reference Desk Database

**www.eduref.org/Eric/**

This is a database of over a million abstracts related to education, which covers a wide swath. You may use the database to locate the actual documents, find various libraries with more data available, or view the documents online if you choose to subscribe to that service.

## Intute

**www.intute.ac.uk/**

It looks like a search engine, feels like a directory, and is in fact a database of websites, each of which has been deemed (by someone who knows) to be one of the best available for purposes of education and research. Based in the United Kingdom, Intute evolved from the Resource Discovery Network and is maintained by a number of universities and institutes.

## Technical Communication Library

**http://tc.eserver.org**
**http://tc.eserver.org/sitemaps/categories.lasso**

This is a site especially for technical writers. It's classic UnderWeb: there are many resources here, but it is unlikely that much of the library's content will show up in the results of most search engines, so you need to poke around a little. They have more than 8,500 articles and entries here, organized under various subjects and groupings. The second URL is a page where you can browse (or search) through the subjects; click on one, and the resources under that subject are listed. In this case, a resource could be an article, it could be a list of links, it could be a pointer to other databases like this one. Nice interface, too.

## Topica

**http://lists.topica.com**

The Internet has many mailing lists for many newsletters, for people who are interested in many different subjects. At Topica, nestled somewhere in the advertising, you will see a box that says, "Choose from Thousands of Newsletters and Discussions." Clicking on the subject headings will lead you to pages with even more subjects, which will eventually lead you to (just like it says) thousands of newsletters on thousands of subjects, all of which you can subscribe to, or otherwise access.

## ibiblio

**www.ibiblio.org**

An excellent digital archive. Most stuff is not directly related to job-hunting, of course, but who knows what you may, some day, need to know? Lots of data about language, literature, history, and science.

## Academic Info

**www.academicinfo.net**

Also not necessarily related, at least directly, to the job hunt, but I list this site in a number of places in this book, for a number of reasons. In this case, if you need to research a subject—history, science, engineering, health—this is a great place to go. In the middle of the page you'll see Subject Gateways, with links to various subjects. Unless you have some time on your hands, don't go here if you have even the smallest amount of curiosity about the world around you. There is so much good stuff, you will probably be wandering for a while.

## DirectSearch

**www.freepint.com/gary/direct.htm**

This is a collection of specialty databases and search engines, compiled by Gary Price, coauthor of *The Invisible Web* (Cyberage, 2001), a classic in the field. The site is somewhat eclectic, and certainly not complete in any sense, but there are a lot of links to data sources you would probably not find any other way.

## U.S. Patent and Trademark Office

**www.uspto.gov/patft**

Huge databases containing trademark information and patent data going back to 1790. As with many UnderWeb locations, the site is spare and utilitarian, and you may need a little time to feel comfortable here. Note that Google also has patent info.

### Delphion $$

**www.delphion.com**

As you know, I don't usually recommend fee-based services on the Internet, but if you need to do intellectual property research the world over, this is hard to beat. The database is huge, the search tools extensive, the quality of data excellent. It's not cheap, but the data here may be worth it for you.

## OTHER DATA FORMS

Search engines often ignore page content that is not written in HTML, but that doesn't mean you should. For instance, try this with Google:

> career change older employee filetype:doc

This would return the addresses of any documents written in Microsoft Word on that subject. Or instead of "doc," try "pdf" for Adobe Acrobat files, "xls" for Excel spreadsheets, and so on.

Adobe Acrobat files—that is, those whose filenames have a "pdf" extension—can be a gold mine of information. (For example, it's a standard format for company reports.) Standard search engines won't always read Acrobat files, and for those that do, size limits can make the contents partially or completely invisible. It has been reported that Google will not index the data in files, pdf or otherwise, that are larger than 100KB to 500KB (figures vary by source and file type). This means that for some search engines, if a file is too large, then the data inside the file may as well not exist.

But even though the search engine doesn't know what's in such a file, it still knows where the file is. You can still find these documents, using this technique, and open them yourself.

## ARTICLES ABOUT INTERNET RESEARCH

If you would like more information about performing general research on the Internet, take a look at the following articles:

### Finding Information on the Internet

**www.lib.berkeley.edu/TeachingLib/Guides/Internet/FindInfo.html**

From the library at U.C. Berkeley, this is the best single article I've found on Internet research.

### Deep Web White Paper

**http://brightplanet.com/technology/deepweb.asp#Introduction**

From BrightPlanet, this is a really good one as well. Excellent source list of references and links.

### The Invisible Web

**www.lib.berkeley.edu/TeachingLib/Guides/Internet/InvisibleWeb.html**

Another excellent article from the Berkeley library, which explains more about the UnderWeb and how to find resources there.

### Searching the Internet: Recommended Sites and Search Techniques

**www.internettutorials.net/search.html**

Also good.

## RESEARCHING CAREERS—ARTICLES

We can now turn toward research that is more focused on the job hunt itself. The first task on our list involves researching various careers; here are a few articles on the subject:

### High-Earning Workers Who Don't Have a Bachelor's Degree

**http://stats.bls.gov/opub/ooq/1999/fall/art02.pdf**

### Top Jobs for the Future

**www.careerplanner.com/Career-Articles/Top_Jobs.htm**

### Top Ten Jobs for People Who . . .

**www.princetonreview.com/cte/articles/plan/tenjobs.asp**

### Ten Hottest Careers for College Grads

**www.collegeboard.com/student/csearch/majors_careers/236.html**

### Ten Hottest Careers in Australia

**www.jobsearchexpress.com/jobsearchexpress/articles/careers/ten-hottest-careers.html**

Don't you wonder what they would name these articles if we all had six fingers on each hand?

### Best Jobs in America

**http://money.cnn.com/magazines/moneymag/bestjobs/2007/**

Articles with information about what jobs are best for various population groups—over fifty, parents returning to the work force, those leaving the military, and so forth.

## RESEARCHING CAREERS—WEBSITES

At this point, you should have some idea of the skills you want to use, and the fields of endeavor in which you would prefer to use them. Thus enlightened, you can use the following sites to help you come up with some job titles and descriptions.

### Bureau of Labor Statistics

**www.bls.gov**

What is happening in certain industries? What is the turnover for certain careers? The outlook for hiring over the next few years? Regional data? National data? Costs of employment? Demographics of the labor force? Fatalities on the job? Wages by area and occupation? International labor data? And on and on.

*Anything* having to do with work that the government wants to know is here—and trust me, they want to know *everything*. Note also the next two entries.

## The Occupational Outlook Handbook

**www.bls.gov/oco/**

This is the bible of occupational fields, put out by the U.S. Department of Labor, Bureau of Labor Statistics; updated every two years; and the obvious place to begin in researching particular occupational fields. Here you will find descriptions of "what workers do on the job, working conditions, the training and education needed, earnings, and expected job prospects in a wide range of occupations."

## Dictionary of Occupational Titles

**www.occupationalinfo.org**

Long considered the career counselor's bible, the dictionary is available in its entirety at this site.

## O*Net OnLine

**http://online.onetcenter.org**
**http://online.onetcenter.org/find/**
**http://online.onetcenter.org/skills/**

Here at the Occupational Information Network is the cyberspace version of the *Dictionary of Occupational Titles*. The second page allows you to find occupations based on a number of criteria. The third page is specifically for translating skills into a job; check off the skills that you have, and the site returns job titles.

## Vocational Information Center

**www.khake.com/page5.html**

What a great page! Links to almost *everything*. Job market information, economic outlook, licensing authorities, and so on. Terrific.

## America's Career InfoNet

**www.acinet.org**

Part of CareerOneStop, the U.S. government's online career resource network, this is another excellent place to research occupations and career fields, using data from the U.S. Department of Labor.

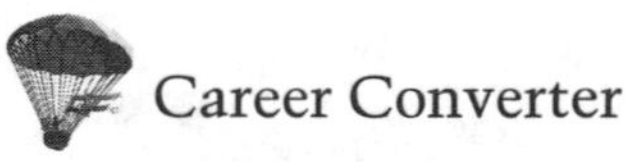

### Career Converter

**http://content.monstertrak.monster.com/tools/careerconverter/**

A neat little utility from the Monster College Center: you input your major (or area of interest), and the utility gives you a list of possible job titles. Obviously, you can use this for more than was originally intended; the utility contains a pretty good list of job titles.

### Job and Career Resources for Teenagers

**www.quintcareers.com/teen_jobs.html**

From the Quintessential Careers site, an excellent collection of articles and links for teenagers looking for employment.

### The Creative Group

**www.creativegroup.com/TCG/TCGJobs/**

On this page is a list of job titles in the graphic arts industry, with links to definitions for them.

## INFORMATIONAL INTERVIEWING

The informational interview is a low-stress way of making contacts and conducting research about fields that interest you. It is not an online activity, but here are some online articles about it. The latest edition of *What Color Is Your Parachute?* has much more about informational interviews.

### Informational Interviewing

**http://danenet.wicip.org/jets/jet-9407-p.html**

This important technique is explained and discussed at this site. Although the site makes this technique a bit more complex than it needs to be, it still provides a good overview.

### Informational Interviewing Tutorial

**www.quintcareers.com/informational_interviewing.html**

Another Quintessential Careers home run: one of the best and most complete articles (actually, it is a series of articles) available on the subject.

## RESEARCHING INDUSTRIES

Once you've identified the fields and industries that interest you, you will want to look at industry news, trends, professional pay scales, names of associations in the field, schedules of meetings or networking events, and so on. You can start with these:

### CareerOneStop

**www.acinet.org/industry/default.aspx?id=8&nodeid=8**

This page at the U.S. government's career website is very useful for gathering industry information.

### CEO Express

**www.ceoexpress.com**

Links to all kinds of business resources: the financial and business industry press, international business, trade associations; lots of stuff here.

### Yahoo! Professional Organizations

**http://dir.yahoo.com/Business_and_Economy/organizations/professional**

A good way to find out more about a particular field is to go to the website of its association or professional organization. Many such are listed here.

### WEDDLE's Professional Associations

**www.weddles.com/associations/index.htm**

An excellent list of professional associations, from the site of one of the masters of the job hunt and the Web.

### Associations on the Net

**www.ipl.org/div/aon/**

A large directory of industry associations.

### Association Directory

**www.asaecenter.org/Directories/AssociationSearch.cfm**

This allows you to search for various industry associations by name, industry, geographic area, or association type.

### Thomas Global Register: Industry and Professional Organizations

**www.thomasglobal.com/main/industrylinks.asp?bhcp=1**

At this page on the Thomas Global Register site, you will find an extensive list of trade and professional organizations.

### The Career Guide to Industries

**www.bls.gov/oco/cg/home.htm**

Companion to the *Occupational Outlook Handbook* (listed earlier under "Researching Careers"). Whereas the *Handbook* looks at jobs from an occupational point of view, the Career Guide to Industries "provides information on available careers by industry, including the nature of the industry, working conditions, employment, occupations in the industry, training and advancement, earnings and benefits, employment outlook, and lists of organizations that can provide additional information."

## MOVING, RELOCATING, AND RESEARCHING COMMUNITIES

Once you have identified the type of industries that interest you, you should take a look at where in the world you want to live and work. It may be that there are no industries that interest you where you currently live, or you may take this as an excellent time to relocate to a part of the country where you have always wanted to live.

You can research any place you want, simply by typing its name into your search engine's query line, along with any terms to help focus the search. Press Enter and see what turns up. Also, try the sites listed in this section. Don't skimp on this aspect of the job hunt—a dream job is meaningless if you must live in a nightmare city or endure a three-hour commute.

### Jobmaps

**http://jobmaps.us/**

Jobmaps is a combination of the Indeed job search engine and Google Maps. Input a job title and a city or state (also works with "US" for the entire country) and you'll get a map showing where Indeed's listings for that job title are located.

## The Best Places to Live in America

**http://money.cnn.com/best/bplive**

Want to move to a new city, town, or country place? Wonder which one is best for you? *Money* magazine's site has not only the statistics, weather, housing costs, and so on for more than twelve hundred cities around the United States, but also a wonderful interactive feature called "Find Your Best Place." You rank nine criteria by how important they are to you, and the search engine will tell you which cities (or places) fit the criteria as you ranked them. You can specify how many cities you want, and it will give you the answers with data about each place, including a "cost of living comparator" (at **http://cgi.money.cnn.com/tools/costofliving/costofliving.html**) to help you figure out whether you'll be richer or poorer if you move from where you are. If you get too many choices, you can further refine it by ranking a list of sixty-three factors; however, the more factors you check, the more you run the risk of finding out there's no place in the country like that. Wait for heaven.

## CareerJournal.com

**www.careerjournal.com/salaryhiring/indicators/**

Want to move primarily for the sake of finding a job, and wonder where the unemployment is so low that finding a job should be a cinch? This site—from the *Wall Street Journal* folks—lists precisely which U.S. communities had the lowest (and highest) unemployment rates. You know enough to tell yourself that numbers alone don't show the big picture, but hey, it's a start.

And while you're in the neighborhood, the *WSJ* also sponsors the *Real Estate Journal*, which has a section on relocation at **www.realestatejournal.com/relocation**.

## American Journalism Review NewsLink

**http://newslink.org/daynews.html**

Much information on a city can be gleaned from its newspaper (and it seems that the smaller the town, the more this is true). Here you can find links to more than four thousand newspapers, grouped by city and state. The site also has listings of radio and TV stations, magazines, and international publications.

## All You Can Read

**www.allyoucanread.com**

Newspapers from around the world.

## Chambers of Commerce Directory

**http://clickcity.com/index2.htm**

Need to know more about a city or town? Interested in a business located in that city? Start at the chamber of commerce. Here is a good list of city/town chambers of commerce, with links to their websites and email addresses.

## Cell Phone Coverage

**www.cellreception.com/coverage/**

You're moving to a new area and you want to know how the cell phone reception is for the various carriers. Here you'll find complaints and kudos for various cell companies.

## Home Price Records

**www.homepricerecords.com**

If you are moving to a new town and considering buying a home, this site, using Google Maps, will tell you what houses have recently sold for in a given area. Pretty cool.

## Housing Maps

**www.housingmaps.com**

This site gathers rentals, home sales, sublets, and rooms to rent from craigslist and shows where they are located using Google Maps. You can click on an area and get a listing of what is currently available in various price ranges, or choose a price range and see what is available in different areas . . . like that.

## The Weather Channel

**www.weather.com/activities/driving**

In a review of this book's last edition, I received some criticism for listing this site. But if you want climate information about someplace, who is going to know more than the Weather Channel? Historical climate data, long-range forecasts, climate trends. Plus extras: if you want to go visit the town or city in question, you can get a driving forecast, with road conditions, special circumstances, weather at your destination, and so on. Decided to fly there? If you're flying commercial, go to **www.weather.com/activities/travel/businesstraveler/** for destination weather, flight times, and so on. If you have a pilot's license and are flying yourself, get winds aloft, en-route weather, NOTAMs—good site.

## ZipFind Demo

**www.zipfind.net/ZipFindDeluxe.aspx**

ZipFind is a company that sells zip code–oriented software. Because these folks are the wonderful people that they are, they have placed some free utilities on their site for your use. These include a utility that allows you to calculate the distance between any two zip codes; a lookup database to find the zip for any community in the United States; and—the most useful, I think—a utility that tells you what other towns and cities are within various distances of a certain zip code. So if your job is to be in a new city, and you want the names of some of the surrounding suburbs, this is the place to go.

## HomeFair

**www.homefair.com**

## Realtor.com

**www.realtor.com**

This site and HomeFair are both sponsored by the National Association of Realtors. There is a lot of overlap between the sites, but each also has a slightly (maybe more than slightly) different emphasis.

At HomeFair, there are a number of tools for researching communities. For example, say you are moving from a small town to a job in a big city, but you like living in small towns and want to see what other communities near the new job might be to your taste. Use the Community Calculator to see what small towns are within commuting distance. The Moving Calculator helps you see the difference in taxes, insurance, and other financial factors related to moving. The Salary Calculator compares cost-of-living factors, and so on.

Realtor.com has some of the same features but is more about finding a realtor, looking at home listings, checking out mortgage rates, and the like. You can also find information on moving, researching schools where you are moving to, renting an apartment, and more.

## U.S. Census Bureau

**http://factfinder.census.gov/home/saff/main.html?_lang=en**

Well, who knows more about what's going on in the various communities in America than the government? Okay, maybe that's the wrong question. Anyway, this site has an *unbelievable* amount of information. Type in an address and find out more than you thought possible about the town or city, county, people, businesses, housing—very current info, too, not just from the well-known decennial (that's every ten years—work it into a conversation and amaze your friends) census. With all of this data riding on the work the Census Bureau does, it's no wonder they get so testy when you don't fill in the forms they send out.

### Sigalert

**www.sigalert.com**

You know those transponders you can get for your car that allow you to zip through the toll booths and have the toll charged automatically to your credit card? Well, they are also used to track how traffic is moving in certain urban areas around the country. At this site, you can see what commute traffic is like, how fast everyone is moving at various points, which routes are most effective over time, and which areas always seem to have accidents.

### Where the Commuting Nightmares Are

**www.bizjournals.com/edit_special/56.html**

This article from Bizjournals details the best and the worst commutes. There is also a chart ranking sixty-five different areas based on the commute. (Omaha and Buffalo are the best, New York City and Washington, D.C., the worst.)

## FINDING COMPANIES

When looking for companies, organizations, or businesses in your chosen industry and geographical area, one of the best places to start, on or off the Internet, is the yellow pages. I have listed some sites that have yellow pages–type listings; however, you should know that these are not a reproduction of the complete yellow pages phone book you have sitting on your desk. Each online resource is incomplete when compared with the actual, bona fide, phone-company-published yellow pages. (Nor are the secondary yellow pages, published under various names by companies *other* than your phone company, anywhere near as good as the real thing.)

So keep this in mind: your phone book knows more than the Internet yellow pages do about the local businesses in your chosen category. Keep that phone book at your elbow while doing local research. The Internet will, of course, be helpful for the faraway places that your phone book doesn't cover—so long as you remember that it's not going to give you a complete listing of businesses *there*, either. Start by thinking broadly, in a geographical sense, and then move on to the other tools available to you.

### Yellow.com

**www.yellow.com**

From a single form, you can search the SmartPages, Yellow.com, YP.com, Dex-Online, Real Pages, and the Yahoo! directory listings. There's also a zip and area code lookup database, with links to maps, services, and so on.

You can also find people, as the site has a section for white pages lookups at **www.yellow.com/white.html**. There are other pages for doing reverse number lookups and address searches, as well as looking for people on the Web.

### Addresses.Com

**www.addresses.com**

In addition to finding people and businesses, there are reverse email and phone lookups, links to public records, and—just what you wanted!—a database of mailing and email addresses for many celebrities.

### Canada.com

**www.canada.com/findit/findabusiness.html**

Listings for Canada. You can search by city, province, type of business, or name of business.

## MORE ON FINDING COMPANIES

If you need some incentive to help you get through some of this company research, consider this: it can cost a company over $5 a day to list a position through Monster or the other job boards. It costs virtually nothing to list their openings at their own website or to advertise internally or through word of mouth. A 2003 study showed that of those companies that hired through the Internet, 59 percent of their hires were through the company's own website—far more than were hired through internet job boards. As time passes, more and more companies are abandoning the job boards entirely. This means that you must take the active role and find such companies through your own research.

As you discover a company's strengths and weaknesses, you will get a sense of how your skills and abilities can (or, just as importantly, *cannot*) help them. Being able to state a strong case to the person there who has the power to hire depends on thorough research.

## Kompass

**www.kompass.com**

Kompass is a business search engine. Their database lists over two million companies in seventy countries around the world, organized by product, service, and general business category. Not particularly U.S.-centric, but very valuable if you are looking for companies outside the States, and still useful for doing searches within U.S. borders.

## MapQuest

**www.mapquest.com**

More than just a place to get driving directions, this is also a good place to go when you want to find out what businesses are in certain industries in a particular city. For example, to get a list of any oil refiners within fifty miles of Santa Barbara, California, just press the Business Category button, enter "oil refiners" and "santa barbara" and "ca" in the appropriate places—*et voilà*! Pretty neat—and of course, you can then get a map showing you how to get there.

## Vault

**http://vault.com/companies/searchcompanies.jsp**

A good site for locating companies; you can search using various parameters such as industry, city and state (and country), number of employees, and annual revenue.

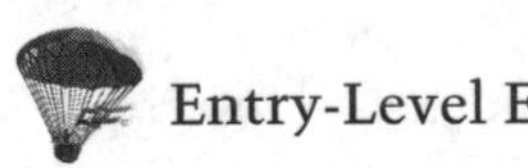

## Entry-Level Employers Search

**www.collegegrad.com/employers/**

From the CollegeGrad website, a database of employers looking for entry-level employees. Obviously, these companies will also hire experienced personnel.

## Career InfoNet Employer Locator

**www.acinet.org/acinet/employerlocator/employerlocator.asp?id=14&nodeid=18**

A database of employers, searchable by industry, occupation, location, and keyword.

## Business.com

**www.business.com**

A large directory of businesses, organized by industry, with links to their home pages. Thousands of public, private, and international companies.

## Yahoo! Company Directories

**http://dir.yahoo.com/Business_and_Economy/Directories/Companies**

Another large directory, organized by industry—thousands of companies, with links to their home pages.

## ThomasNet

**www.thomasnet.com/home.html**

This is the website of the *Thomas Register*, the manufacturer's bible. The site is a great place to do company research. When you want to know what companies are working in what fields, there is no other resource like the *Thomas Register*. This website allows you to find basic company data, such as contact information, number of employees, parent company, and so forth. But the internet version of the *Thomas Register* doesn't have anywhere near the data of the actual published version. When you are researching a company, you really should go down to the library and locate the actual published *Register*.

## Thomas Global Register

**www.tgrnet.com**

What the *Thomas Register* does for the United States, the *Global Register* does for the world—but even the *Global Register*'s database is pretty U.S.-

centric, so if you don't find what you want at the (nonglobal) *Thomas Register* site, come here. You can search by product or company name, or browse the many industries and products listed by category. You have to register to use the site, but all the basic stuff is free.

### Best Companies to Work For

**http://money.cnn.com/magazines/fortune/bestcompanies/2007/index.html**

On the CNNMoney.com website, there is a page with information on what companies are best, according to different criteria. There is even a little application you can use to choose the factors most important to you—number of women, ethnically diverse, turnover rate, and so on—and it returns a list of companies that might fit.

### EmplawyerNet

**www.emplawyernet.com**

The site has a directory of legal recruiters and employers around the country, grouped by city and state.

### Restaurant Source Guide

**www.sourceguides.com/restaurants/index.html**

For those drawn to the food industry, a database of over fifty thousand restaurants organized by state and service type.

## MORE TIPS ON COMPANY RESEARCH

Beyond the sites listed here, there are a number of databases and directories that can help you find companies by industry and location. One approach is to use Google (or any other search engine) to target data on industries and companies.

For example, if you want to find a list of hospitals in Texas, you could go to Google and try this search query:

hospitals texas

In response, you'll get a list of links to pages that list every hospital in Texas. This also works, of course, with Idaho, West Virginia,

Bermuda, and so on; and you can replace "hospital" with "waste treatment center" or "accounting firms" or what have you. Occasionally, you may have to tweak the command slightly, perhaps by adding the word "list" or "database" using the appropriate syntax.

As you do these searches, make notes about the databases and directories you find. Then, when you are researching particular companies or institutions, go back to these and use the "site" command.

For example, one of the hospital directories I found is Hospital Soup, which is primarily a medical jobs database. If you wanted to find the military hospitals in their database, you could use the "site" command along with their URL and the word "military," like this:

site:www.hospitalsoup.com/ military

(Note: you may find that you will need a space after the slash.)

This limits the search to the Hospital Soup website and returns every entry in their database that has "military" in its name. This simple example shows how easy it is to focus your research efforts and save many hours of valuable time.

Remember also the "link" command, mentioned earlier in this chapter, that returns every website that links to the site you are inquiring about. This can be a valuable research strategy because useful websites tend to know about other useful websites. A site that deals in a certain subject will tend to know of others that deal with that subject. So when you find a useful site, find out what other sites link to it; this is one of the most useful search techniques available when doing company research online.

## RESEARCHING SPECIFIC COMPANIES

Once you know the name of an organization or company that looks interesting, you'll of course want to be able to research it, finding out as much as you possibly can before you ever go there for an interview. There are many reasons to do this, but let me give you a few:

- First of all, you may be able to identify problems that a company has and that your skills can solve. Identify the person with the power to hire, explain to them why hiring *you* is in their best interests, and you just may find yourself employed. The depth of research this requires may be beyond what you can get just sitting at your computer, but you can certainly get the basics, as well as identify your next steps, through intelligent research on the Internet.

- If you have a job interview, learning all that you can about that organization reassures the interviewer that you cared enough to learn about the company before coming in for the interview. This involves research at its most basic level—the company's primary business, address, number of employees, and so on. The Internet is good for this basic sort of research.

- You are also researching a company in order to protect yourself from making a horrible mistake—taking a job that you'll soon have to quit because of something that you didn't know or didn't bother to find out before you started there. The purpose of this sort of research is to find these time bombs *before* you agree to take the job.

  In such a case, what do you want to know? Well, think of the jobs you've had in the past and try to recall the moment when you were about to leave that job—your decision or theirs. What was it, at that moment, you wished you had known before you took the job? This will give you your research topics. Likely items include the following:

1. What the real goals of the company were, instead of the puffery they put in the annual report.

2. What the corporate culture was like there: cold and clammy or warm and appreciative.

3. What timelines the company conducted its work under and whether they were flexible or inflexible.

4. What the job was really like.

5. Whether the skills you care the most about in yourself were really employed. Or was all that talk about "your skills" just window dressing to lure you there—and you, with your rich people skills, ended up spending your time pushing paper?
6. What the boss was like to work for. Ditto for your immediate supervisor(s).
7. What your coworkers were like: easy to get along with or difficult? And who was which?
8. How close the company or organization was to having to lay off people, or how tight your department's budget was.

If those were the questions in your past, then they are also the questions for your future. If an organization interests you, these are the things you will want to research before you get a job offer there—*if* you get a job offer there.

Can the Internet help with this kind of research? It depends on how deep you want to go and, in some cases, how much money you want to spend—but spending money is no guarantee that you will find out all you want to know. Face it: there's only so much the Internet can do. If you're going to go deeper, and find out the information you really want to know, you're going to need to supplement this online research with some offline research—meaning you'll have to go talk to people, using your contacts, to thoroughly research the companies that interest you.

But the following sites will certainly help; you should also check the job board descriptions in chapter 3, many of which have employer databases, and the resources in chapter 4, such as Spoke and Business .com, where you will also find extensive company information.

## Competitive Intelligence—Get Smart!

**www.fastcompany.com/online/14/intelligence.html**

This is an introductory article, written to describe what people in business can learn about rivals by skimming the Internet—but for job-hunters, the most helpful parts are those that tell you how to find out more about companies that interest you.

## Tutorial: Researching Companies Online

**www.learnwebskills.com/company/**

Not a huge amount of depth, but if you don't know where to start, this is the place.

## Company Research Guide—Rutgers University

**www.libraries.rutgers.edu/rul/rr_gateway/research_guides/busi/company.shtml**

An excellent guide to researching companies online and off.

## Chambers of Commerce Directory

**http://clickcity.com/index2.htm**

In addition to information on living conditions, a city's chamber of commerce often has good information about the business climate there, as well as data on various businesses and local professional associations. Go to this page for a list of chambers, with website and email addresses.

## Bizjournals

**www.bizjournals.com/search.html**

This site gathers together publications from the business press from all over the country. You can search the archive for any mention of the company (or industry or person) that you are interested in; there's a lot here. You must register, but access is free. There are other goodies on this site as well.

## Refdesk.com

**www.refdesk.com/paper.html**

You will be amazed at how much industry and company information you can get from the newspaper—and very little of it will be available through the normal search engines. To access this data, you need to go to the websites of the newspapers themselves; the newspapers that service a company's local area are particularly valuable. Refdesk—an amazing site—has a page here that links to newspapers in every state and around the world. There is a ton of information in Refdesk's archive and even more at the websites of the newspapers themselves. Also, take a look at the Quick Reference resources at **www.refdesk.com/instant.html**.

## Securities and Exchange Commission

**www.sec.gov**
**www.sec.gov/edgar.shtml**

All public corporations, domestic and foreign, who do business in the United States are required to file all kinds of forms and papers with the SEC. All such filings, and more, end up in the SEC's EDGAR database (which stands for Electronic Data Gathering, Analysis, and Retrieval). EDGAR is huge, and it can take a little while to get the hang of using it effectively, but what a tremendous resource. Note the tutorial and overview at **www.sec.gov/investor/pubs/edgarguide.htm**.

## SEDAR

**www.sedar.com**

The Canadian equivalent of EDGAR, this is a database of filings by publicly traded companies operating on Canadian soil.

## Yahoo! Finance

**http://finance.yahoo.com/search**

Enter company name, stock symbol, and so on, and get back a profile of the company. Or, if you want to find companies with a word in their name, enter that word, and all companies in the database with that word in their name will be listed. (Not foolproof, but this is one way to find companies in a certain industry: for example, enter "finance" or "aircraft," and every company that uses that word in its name will come up.) There are lots of companies in the database and many ways of getting to them, though it will take a little exploring for you to find them all.

## WetFeet Company Profiles

**www.wetfeet.com/research/companies.asp**

A directory of companies, organized by industry. Not the most complete listing available, but for the companies that are listed, you'll find profiles with sales data, number of employees, office locations, company and industry overviews, and so on.

## 4,000 Company Web Pages

**http://interbiznet.com/hunt/companies**

From Interbiznet, a listing of the web pages of four thousand different companies.

## The Virtual Chase

**www.virtualchase.com/topics/company_information_index.shtml**

Tons of links to resources for researching companies in various industries. When you are stuck and need an idea of how to mine company info, browse through this list.

## Database of Company Profiles

**www.gsb.stanford.edu/jacksonlibrary/articles/databases/db_comdir.html**

A terrific list of databases containing company information. Unless you are online from Stanford, you will be denied access to some but allowed in others. Give them a try; it's a gold mine.

## Corporate Information

**www.corporateinformation.com**

Although detailed information requires a subscription, this website is a good place to find basic data on thousands of corporations around the world. This includes business description, recent stock performance, annual sales, number of employees, and major competitors.

## UBC: Researching Private Companies

**http://toby.library.ubc.ca/subjects/subjpage2.cfm?id=273**

This is a great page from the University of British Columbia, useful for researching Canadian companies, with links to many resources.

## CNNMoney

**http://money.cnn.com**

There are a lot of resources at the site of *Money* and *Fortune* magazines, including company profiles, best companies to work for, and many timely articles for job-hunters.

## The World's 2,000 Largest Public Companies

**www.forbes.com/2006/03/29/06f2k_worlds-largest-public-companies_land.html**

Much of the data here is stock oriented, but there are interesting profiles as well.

## Fast Company—Company Database

**http://fcke.fastcompany.com**

*Fast Company* magazine has a database of "the world's most interesting and innovative companies." You can search by name, location, or industry, or browse alphabetically.

## Monster Company Boulevard

**http://company.monster.com**

A number of companies here, though little depth in the company-generated profiles. Naturally, there are links to any jobs those companies are currently listing with Monster.

## Europages

**www.europages.com**

A basic listing of companies in Europe—550,000 of them, in thirty-three countries. Not much depth to the actual company data, but it's very handy to be able to browse by industry or to search for companies with *this* many employees, in *these* countries, working in *this* field.

## BuildFind

**www.buildfind.com**

This is a site for researching firms in the construction industry. You can search by company, product, project, or person.

## The Wall Street Journal $$

**http://online.wsj.com**

I don't recommend too many websites that charge for their services, but if you are job-hunting in the corporate world, you should have a really good reason for *not* subscribing. The cost is reasonable—around $79 a year—and occasionally there will be free trial offers you can take advantage of.

## LexisNexis $$

**www.lexisnexis.com**

## Factiva $$

**www.factiva.com**

### Dialog $$

**www.dialog.com**

LexisNexis, the venerable search company, is not free, and if you do a lot of research here, you can run up quite a bill. But it has one of the best research databases around, as do the other two listed here. If you are not finding what you need through free services, then you might consider using LexisNexis. Professional researchers often use the two other fee services, Factiva and Dialog, along with LexisNexis. I personally think that before you jump from free services to fee services, you should stop and see what your contacts and a little networking can dig up. Not only is this often cheaper—maybe a few lunch bills, versus nudging up against the limits on your credit cards—but it also gives you the opportunity to turn off that confounded machine and poke your head out, blinking myopically, to spend some time in the real world.

### Dun and Bradstreet $$

**www.dnb.com**

The king of business report companies does not have much for free on its site, but it does have basic company contact info. If you want to dig deeper into a company, you can buy D & B's report about that company.

## SALARIES

Whether you are researching industries and fields or mulling over a specific job offer, you will need to know as much about the money involved as possible. Use a number of sites and average the data you get. Your goal is to find specific salary data for that job *in the city where you will be working*. Salaries vary widely in different parts of the country; make sure you look up cost-of-living data, which will often explain the wider swings.

### CareerJournal—Salary Data and Hiring Trends

**www.careerjournal.com/salaryhiring**

Salary tables and hiring data for hundreds of fields; also shows different pay levels within careers for more senior levels. There's a Salary Calculator for comparing pay levels between different areas, as well as a Salary Search: what does *this* job pay in *this* particular area? The site also displays the latest news about salaries and salary trends in various segments of the job market, culled from *The Wall Street Journal* daily. These articles are very current and also archived going back quite a ways. Excellent, like everything on this site.

## The Salary Expert

**www.salaryexpert.com**

When you need the best information, you go to an expert; and if you need the best salary information, I suppose you go to the Salary Expert. Lots of stuff on the subject here, including a Salary Report for hundreds of job titles, varying by area, skill level, and experience. Also has one of the salary calculators mentioned earlier.

## Salary.com

**www.salary.com**

Probably the most visited of all the salary-specific job sites; a few years ago they were getting over two million visitors per month, and I doubt it is any fewer now. If it has to do with salaries, it's here; many other salary sites use resources from this one.

## Payscale

**www.payscale.com**

Do you want to see how your current salary compares with the same job in other areas? Is a salary offer above or below industry averages? This is where you check.

## JobStar Salary Surveys

**www.jobstar.org/tools/salary/sal-surv.cfm**

One of the best lists of salary surveys on the Internet; other sites claiming to have big salary surveys actually just link to this one, the mother of all salary surveys—more than three hundred of them. Before you choose a career, before you hunt for a job, before you go in for the hiring interview—maybe even before you start sixth grade—you should know this information!

## The Real Rate Survey

**www.realrates.com/survey.htm**

On this bulletin board, "computer consultants" (very broadly defined) post what they made on their last job or contract, and where that was. You can search this completely up-to-date site by salary, location, platform, and so on. Also includes a section called Tips and Gotchas, with short blurbs on improving your consulting business and avoiding pitfalls.

### Salary Source $$

**www.salarysource.com**

If the free sites don't give you what you want, you can always pay for the info, and maybe get more up-to-date data. Salary Source offers information services starting at $19.95.

## SELF-EMPLOYED AND HOME BUSINESS

Some people are just happier working for themselves, even if the hours are long and the pay is short. Try these sites for more on self-employment:

### Business Owner's Toolkit

**www.toolkit.com/small_business_guide/index.aspx**

Yikes, but there is a lot of information here for the small business owner. Everything about your business: starting, planning, financing, marketing, hiring, managing, getting government contracts, taxes—all that stuff.

### Small Business Administration

**www.sba.gov**

The SBA was established to help people start, manage, and grow small businesses—but bear in mind that it defines "small business" as one with fewer than five hundred employees (it could be called the "Almost All Businesses Administration"). Lots of useful stuff here; also, check out the "Starting a Business" resources at **www.sba.gov/starting_business/index.html**.

## The Business Owner's Idea Café

**http://businessownersideacafe.com**

Great site for the small business owner.

## Startup Journal

**www.startupjournal.com**

*The Wall Street Journal* brings its considerable resources to bear on this site for the entrepreneur. Many articles, how-tos, advice, and resources for the business owner.

## Free Agent Nation

**www.fastcompany.com/online/12/freeagent.html**

The workplace is changing dramatically. Among these changes is the fact that for some, self-employment has become a broader concept than it was in another age. The concept can now include not only those who own their own business, but also free agents. These are independent contractors who work for several clients; temps and contract employees who work each day through temporary agencies; limited-time-frame workers who work only for a set time, as on a project, then move on to another company; consultants; and so on. This is a fascinating article to help you decide if you want to be part of this trend, on the site of the popular magazine *Fast Company.*

## Working Solo

**www.workingsolo.com**
**www.workingsolo.com/resources/resources.html**

Working Solo is a good site for the home or small business worker. The best stuff on this site is at the second URL.

## A Home-Based Business Online

**www.ahbbo.com**
**www.ahbbo.com/articles.html**

A great site, with lots of information for you if you want to learn about home-based businesses. There are over a hundred articles at the second address.

## Nolo Law Center for Small Business

**www.nolo.com/lawcenter/index.cfm/catID/19B45DBF-E85F-4A3D-950E3E07E32851A7**

Nolo Press publishes a lot of do-it-yourself law books; this is the part of its website that offers legal resources for the small business person. Really good.

## Entrepreneur.com

**www.entrepreneur.com/magazine/entrepreneur/index.html**

*Entrepreneur* magazine's website has lists of home-based businesses, start-up ideas, how to raise money, shoestring start-ups, small business myths, a franchise and business opportunity site-seeing guide, and a lot more. Currently, you are allowed access to the magazine's archives (at **www.entrepreneur.com/entrepreneur/archive/index.html**), with full text of many articles, stretching back to January of 1997. (This complete, no-fee archive access is unusual for most magazines.) Many resources and articles for the self-employed, home businesses, franchises—cool stuff.

## Jobs and Moms: Work at Home

**www.jobsandmoms.com/work_at_home.html**

Another article at a popular women's site.

## Work-at-Home Schemes

**www.ftc.gov/bcp/edu/pubs/consumer/invest/inv14.shtm**

Not everyone using the Internet is as nice as you and me; there are even people in the world who might try to take advantage of a trusting nature. Here is an article to help you protect yourself.

## Top 10 Work-at-Home and Home-Based Business Scams

**www.scambusters.org/work-at-home.html**

A good article from Scambusters.org.

## PART-TIME, CONTRACT, AND TEMPORARY WORK

For the most part, I don't advocate people applying for typical temp jobs through the Internet; you will likely have better luck by going, in person, to your local agency such as Kelly, Manpower, and so on. To find your local agencies, use American Staffing Association (see below) or go to MapQuest (**www.mapquest.com**) and type "temp agency" under Business Category.

But as I said, "for the most part." It's not like a *rule* or anything. Here are some sites and articles related to temporary, part-time, and contract work:

### The Contract Employee's Handbook

**www.cehandbook.com/cehandbook/htmlpages/ceh_main.html**

This is an immensely useful handbook, covering every facet of doing temporary or contract work. The site also has a contract employee's newsletter. It's sponsored by the Professional Association of Contract Employees.

### Temp Jobs

**http://jobsearch.about.com/od/tempjobs/Temporary_Jobs_and_Agencies.htm**

From About.com, there are links here to articles about finding temp work, whether it's right for you, and so on.

### American Staffing Association

**www.americanstaffing.net/jobseekers/find_company.cfm**

Best way to find a temp agency using the Internet. Indicate your area and the kind of work you want, and it kicks back a list—sometimes a very *long* list—of temp agencies near you.

### SnagAJob

**www.snagajob.com**

Part-time, restaurant, hourly, summer jobs—listings, resources, guidance, advice. Youth oriented, but not exclusively.

### Directory of Contract Staffing Firms

**www.cjhunter.com/dcsf/view_some.html?SearchType=complete**

A *huge* listing of firms that hire consultants and contract employees.

### Backdoorjobs.com

**www.backdoorjobs.com**

This site is mostly aimed at young people who are looking for summer situations, temporary jobs, maybe something outdoors, maybe something overseas for a little while; jobs are listed, and there is a sampling of advice from Landes's excellent book, *The Back Door Guide to Short-Term Job Adventures* (Ten Speed Press, 2005). Basically, the author wants you to buy his book (and it's a good book); there's also a lot of useful information and news of opportunities online here.

### Summerjobs.com

**www.summerjobs.com/jobSeekers/resources/links.html**

This is the links page at Summerjobs.com. There are a number of really useful resources here, including Travel and Adventure, Immigration and Visas, and job sites for overseas and resort employment.

## NONPROFITS AND SOCIAL CONSCIENCE

Here are some sites for those interested in careers with nonprofits:

### A Professional Advisor's Guide to Working with Nonprofit Organizations

**www.pgdc.com/usa/item/?itemID=223724**

An extensive and informative article.

### Careers in Nonprofits

**www.bc.edu/offices/careers/careers/careerfields/nonprofits.html**

From the website of Boston College, this is the best page I have found on the Web dealing with this subject; great resources, good links.

## GuideStar: The National Database of Nonprofit Organizations

**www.guidestar.org**

First stop if you're looking to identify prospective nonprofits to work for. Though the site offers fee-based services as well, you may access its database at the GuideStar EZ level for free, where there is at least basic data on over a million U.S. nonprofit organizations.

## Idealist—Action without Borders

**www.idealist.org**

This site has some wonderful lists, categorized by field, state, and country (the directory is worldwide, covering 120 countries). It also lists other nonprofit directories that are on the Web.

## About.com: Nonprofit Charitable Organizations

**http://nonprofit.about.com**

About.com's list of nonprofits.

## The Foundation Center

**http://foundationcenter.org/findfunders/**

Lists and links to nonprofits with a web presence.

## ExecSearches.com

**www.execsearches.com**

ExecSearches is a specialty job site; one of those specialties is placing people in jobs at nonprofit organizations.

## The Nonprofit Career Network $$

**www.nonprofitcareer.com**

One way to go if you are looking for a career in the nonprofit sector or are looking to further the same. The site charges $40 to list your resume for one year, which maybe says something about its confidence in resumes producing quick hires. There are other resources here as well; for instance, a list of nonprofit organizations. Though not the largest database around, it's still worth checking out.

# WORK FOR MINORITIES

## IMDiversity

**www.imdiversity.com**

The best of the sites for minorities. Besides the standard resume- and job-posting facilities, the site is divided into "villages," with resources and articles of special interest for African Americans, Native Americans, Hispanic Americans, Asian Americans, and other minorities. The Career Center page is well done, and there is much here that is of value to anyone, regardless of ancestry.

## LatPro

**www.latpro.com/USER/resources/links/index.php**

From this highly regarded site, which bills itself as "the essential job board for Hispanic and bilingual professionals," comes one of the best resource links pages to be found on an internet job site, regardless of focus. Many of the links lead to Hispanic resources in the United States as well as in Central and South America. For those who are thinking of relocating outside the United States into the Spanish-speaking world, there are links to education and job-hunting resources as well as networking and newspaper sites.

## HireDiversity.com

**www.hirediversity.com**

This is a job- and resume-posting site that caters to those interested in encouraging racial diversity in the workplace.

## Job-Hunting after Thirty-Five

**www.stc.org/intercom/PDFs/2002/20020708_20-22.pdf**

It's not that the elderly are a minority, exactly; there sure seem to be a lot of them. But if any group is routinely discriminated against in the job hunt more, with less thought, I don't know who that is. (You might argue African Americans or Hispanics, but try being an *old* African American or Hispanic.) There are not many resources for the elderly when job-hunting, though this article offers the standard advice that is pretty much echoed by everyone else. I was a little upset to find that the keyword *elderly* in a standard Google search kicked back an article about job-hunting after age thirty-five.

# WORK FOR WOMEN

## WWWomen

**www.wwwomen.com**

WWWomen calls itself "the premier search directory for women online." It has all kinds of resources: women's resources, women's studies, child support help, resources for single parents, mailing lists, and discussion forums (chat rooms). Under the Business heading, it has a huge list of women's associations and women's sites.

## Femina

**www.femina.com/femina/BusinessandFinance/Careers/index.phtml**

Lists "female-friendly sites on the Web." Links to a wide variety of sites of interest to women; this is Femina's careers page, with a pretty impressive list of career-related links.

## Jobs and Moms

**www.jobsandmoms.com**

Resources for the working mother.

## Advancing Women

**www.advancingwomen.com**

This is an international business and career site, dealing with networking, strategy, and employment for women who are looking for a new or better job or ways to advance their career. Features chat rooms and other resources. Allied with CareerBuilder.

# WORK FOR PEOPLE WITH DISABILITIES

## Job-Seeking Skills for People with Disabilities

**www.csun.edu/~sp20558/dis/shcontents.html**

A virtual booklet on job-hunting for people with disabilities, from the Career Center at Cal State Northridge.

## DisabilityInfo.gov

**www.disabilityinfo.gov**

The U.S. government's website for people with disabilities. There is more here than just employment information, of course; for that part of the website, click on the "Employment" subject heading.

## Jobs for the Disabled at Careers.Org

**www.careers.org/jobs/01-55-diversity-employment-disabled.html**

A very good list of links for job-hunters with disabilities.

## Job Accommodation Network

**http://janweb.icdi.wvu.edu**

From the U.S. Department of Labor, JAN is "a free consulting service designed to increase the employability of people with disabilities."

## recruitABILITY

**www.recruit-ability.com**

recruitABILITY is a resume- and job-posting service, specifically targeted toward job-hunters with disabilities and employers who are sensitive to their needs. The service is free to both job hunter and employer.

## Disability and the Workplace: An Internet Primer

**www.ilr.cornell.edu/library/research/subjectGuides/employmentAndDisability.html**

An excellent article/link set from the Cornell University Library.

## Work Support

**http://worksupport.com/Topics/employment.asp**

This is a website with "information, resources, and research about work and disability issues." The page I have provided at the site has an article titled "Job Applicants and the ADA" (the ADA is the Americans with Disabilities Act) and links to more articles about employment issues for people with disabilities. The site has other resources as well.

### WORK*ink*

**www.workink.com**

A Canadian site designed for job-hunters with disabilities, with job- and resume-posting services and other resources. It has extensive—and current—job listings; access is, of course, free.

### Closing the Gap

**www.closingthegap.com/index.lasso**

A site about the use of information technology to help those with disabilities in the workplace.

## WORK IN EDUCATION

### Search for Public Schools

**http://nces.ed.gov/ccd/schoolsearch**

### Search for Private Schools

**http://nces.ed.gov/surveys/pss/privateschoolsearch**

### Search for School Districts

**http://nces.ed.gov/ccd/districtsearch**

Provided by the National Center for Education Statistics, these three databases of schools and districts around the United States are absolutely indispensable if you are looking for a job in K–12 education. You can search using various degrees of specificity; for example, you can look for all schools within twenty miles of a particular zip code. Data returned includes contact info, student count and ethnic mix, other schools in the area, and on and on. Free and *very* helpful.

### Academic Info

**www.academicinfo.net/studentcolleges.html**

Although the site is not always the prettiest to look at, and you need to poke around a little to find what you are looking for, there is an *extensive* list of colleges and universities here, organized by state. It's intended as a guide for students, but this same information is helpful when job-hunting in secondary education; it seems to me that a lab assistant doesn't want to waste her time at a school that doesn't have a laboratory, nor does a professor of astronomy want to teach at a school without an astronomy program.

As I said, it may take a little work, but this site has a lot to offer. For more than the list of colleges and universities, go to the home page at **www.academicinfo.net** and see what you can dig up.

### American School Directory $$

**www.asd.com**

I'm kind of breaking a rule of mine here, in that I don't like to recommend a site that is fee based unless it offers significant free resources—but if you are looking for a teaching job, for a $36 yearly subscription fee (or $9.95 for a one-month trial) you get access to a database of over a hundred thousand school districts in the United States. If the National Center for Education Statistics sites don't yield enough results, you *might* want to consider this site. Along with contact information, the web address, and the number of students and homerooms, there are "wish lists" for each school, indicating the types of teachers needed.

### State Departments of Education

**www.doe.state.in.us/htmls/states.html**

From the Indiana Department of Education, a list of all the other state's departments of education, to help you find job data, certification information for that state, and so on.

### National Directory of Women's Education and Training Programs

**http://associationdigital.com/womenwork/online/directory/default.aspx**

## WORK FOR EX-OFFENDERS

It is stunning to me how little there is online to help ex-offenders find jobs after release. A better bet may be to look for resources with your local probation department. To the degree you are able, talk to those in your shoes who have had employment success; they will often know who is hiring.

Sadly, most of the websites I have found that cater to the ex-offender population are just trying to sell books. Naturally, there are some good books—my favorites are *No One Is Unemployable* (Worknet, 1997), by Angel and Harney, and *The Ex-Offender's Job Hunting Guide* (Impact, 2005), by Krannich and Krannich—but substantial online resources are amazingly thin.

### Ex-Offender Resources & Assistance

**www.hirenetwork.org/resource.html**

A state-by-state directory of resources for ex-offenders reentering the world and the job market.

### Ex-Offender's Resource Pages

**www.angelfire.com/fl4/prison/exresource.html**

A home-grown website with various resources for those seeking to reenter the work force after incarceration.

### Ex-Offender Reentry

**www.exoffenderreentry.com/tips.html**

This site lists a number of articles for the ex-offender job-hunter.

## GRANTS

It may be that the work you most want to do right now is not of the sort for which most companies would be willing to pay you. Perhaps you are a writer, researching a book, or an artist, sculptor, or musician. Maybe you want to run a social program for the homeless or engage in similar selfless endeavors. For those of you who are drawn to pursuits for which our society does not generally pay well, if at all, I present a list of sites where you can investigate the possibility of a grant.

Now, don't think for a moment that this is easy, or a way to get through life without working, or any kind of substitute for a "real job." The chances of *ever* getting a grant are astronomically small, and it is an area where those who know the most about how to get a grant will generally find success sooner than those who are more worthy but ignorant of the process. And, even if you *do* get the grant you are seeking, you must manage the funded project well, account for all money to the penny, and make sure you avoid even the appearance of impropriety. A job is *way* easier.

But people who are drawn to these sorts of things are usually not the types who let little things like extreme difficulty deter them, so here goes:

## Overview of the Grant-Management Process

**www.hhs.gov/grantsnet/OverviewGrantMgtProcess.htm**

The federal government gives away millions of dollars every year. Unless your uncle is a U.S. senator, your only way of getting some of this money is through the competitive grant process. That is, you write and submit a proposal—as do many, many other people—and if your proposal is judged to be one of the more worthy, you receive the money necessary to fund it. Or, more likely, nowhere near enough money to fund it—at least, not from a single source.

This site is arguably the best for accessing the widest variety of government grants. The road to a government grant is often a long and difficult route; with all of the good information here, it would be the first place I would go to start the process.

## Grants and Funding Information Service

**www.lib.washington.edu/gfis/resources/webstuff.html**

This site, and the other sites and databases it points toward, is more academically oriented than others. There is a lot of information as well as links to searchable databases of funding sources.

## Database of Arts Resources

**www.artsnet.org/databases**

If you are an artist looking for funding, this is probably the first internet resource you should turn to. Includes an excellent searchable database of funding sources.

## Grants.gov

**www.grants.gov**

Partnered with the U.S. Department of Health and Human Services, this site is the only point of access, they say, for more than nine hundred grant programs. There is also much good information here on how to apply, how to write a proposal, and so on.

## ED.gov

**www.ed.gov/fund/landing.jhtml?src=rt**

The U.S. Department of Education will provide over $40 billion, in the coming year, in the form of grants for various purposes. Most will go to school districts and educational institutions; some will go to individuals for education and training.

## HUD Grants

**www.hud.gov/grants/index.cfm**

More government money, this time from Housing and Urban Development.

## National Endowment for the Arts

**http://arts.endow.gov**

You've heard of it; everyone else has, too.

## SRA International

**www.srainternational.org/newweb/grantsweb/index.cfm**

At the website of the Society of Research Administrators International, there is information on public and private funding sources for those in the research community.

## Art Deadlines List

**www.artdeadlineslist.com**

Announcements of art grants, organized by deadline.

## Art A to Z: Artist Grants

**www.antiquesatoz.com/artatoz/grant.htm**

Another good place to go if you are an artist in need of a grant to pursue your art. The site also has many resources for artists in general.

## EVALUATING THE DATA

Once you have found the online information you seek, how do you evaluate it? The Internet has leveled the playing field for everyone from the largest corporations to the smallest hoaxer. In many cases, the source of the data—whose website it is on, the newsgroup it is from, or the writer of the email—will tell you a lot about how trustworthy that data is. For cases that are less clear-cut, there are five criteria to use when evaluating data from the Internet:

- Authority: *Who* put the information here? Who wrote it? Why?
- Accuracy: *How much* is verifiable? What were the writer's sources?
- Objectivity: *Why* is the material here? Who supports the site? How does the information relate to any site advertising?
- Currency: *How old* is the information? Can it be dated at all?
- Appearance: *What* does the site look like? Professional? How is the data presented? Free of tyPos and speling erorrs?

To learn more about evaluating web data:

Evaluating Information Found on the Internet
**www.library.jhu.edu/researchhelp/general/evaluating/**

## IN CLOSING

One of the problems with doing your job-hunt research on the Internet (or . . . writing a book about it) is that you can find so many interesting side paths. This can easily divert you from your job hunt for weeks, while giving yourself the illusion that you are hard at work: "Hey, what do you mean I'm not working my job hunt? I was online for six hours yesterday."

When doing your research on the Internet, bring loads of self-discipline. You must know exactly what it is you want to find: make a research plan, write it out, and stick with it. Set yourself a time limit for your data search; don't exceed it. If you've tried to find the data online, and it just isn't there, stop, and try some other methods to mine the data. With time, you will get a better idea of what can and cannot be found online.

Just make sure that all of your surfing—I mean, research—is leading you toward your goal. You're looking for a *job*, remember?

In this, and all your other endeavors, I wish you the best that life and a benevolent Creator can give you.

# SOURCES

## Introduction

. . . your chances of finding a job are less than 10 percent: U.S. Department of Labor, Bureau of Labor Statistics **www.bls.gov/home.htm.**

## Chapter One

Internet usage statistics: **www.internetworldstats.com** and particularly **www.internetworldstats.com/stats2.htm**—their sources include Nielsen/NetStats and ITC.

17 million people logged on to career sites on the Internet: Nielsen/NetRatings, **www.nielsen-netratings.com/pr/pr_030516.pdf**.

Internet use, job hunt statistics: Pew Internet and American Life Project: **www.pewinternet.org**. Article about: **www.clickz.com/stats/markets/professional/article.php/1437221**; see also U.S. Department of Labor, Bureau of Labor Statistics, **www.bls.gov/home.htm**.

Usenet as part of the Internet: Technically, Usenet is not part *of* the Internet but is accessible *through* the Internet. Practically speaking, there is no difference.

DHMO: *Scientific American*, June 2004, page 113; see also **www.dhmo.org**.

8 percent of new hires: Employment Management Association's 2000 "Cost Per Hire and Staffing Metrics Survey," as reported in *Weddle's* 8/1/00.

2003 study of companies that hired through the Internet: CareerXRoads study, published in its newsletter 1/31/03.

2003 study, 61 percent found jobs through contacts: Bernard Haldane Associates Internet Job Report, conducted by Taylor Nelson Sofres Intersearch, reported by Andrea Coombes, CBS **Marketwatch.com** 1/23/2003.

Supersites/Internet job-hunters: Nielsen/NetRatings report, June 2004, and 7/16/04 news release: "U.S. Job Recovery Pushes 30 Percent Growth for Online Career Sites," **http://biz.yahoo.com/prnews/040716/sff017_1.html**.

## Chapter Four

2003 study shows 60 percent of new hires through referrals and the Internet: CareerXRoads Third Annual Source of Hires Study, January 2004, Gerry Crispin and Mark Mehler, **www.careerxroads.com**.

8 percent of new hires: Employment Management Association's 2000 "Cost Per Hire and Staffing Metrics Survey," as reported in *Weddle's* 8/1/00.

We each know 250 people: "The Law of 250," **www.collegegrad.com/jobsearch/8-1.shtml**.

## Chapter Six

MetaCrawler mixes sponsored results with "real" results: **www.lib.berkeley.edu/TeachingLib/Guides/Internet/MetaSearch.html**.

The five criteria for evaluating search results: **www.Widener.Edu/Wolfgram-Memorial-Library/Webevaluation/Inform.htm** and **www.Sofweb.Vic.Edu.Au/Internet/Research.htm**.

Yahoo! has its own search engine; Teoma, Alta Vista, others mix paid results: **http://news.netcraft.com/archives/2004/04/23/desperately_seeking_web_search_20.html**.

# INDEX

## D



## E

## F



## G



## H



## I

## J



## K

## L



## M



## N



## O

## P



## Q



## R

## S



## T



## U

## V



## W



## Y



## Z

# ABOUT THE AUTHORS

MARK EMERY BOLLES has worked as a musical instrument maker, computer programmer, musician, and technical writer and is an expert on using the Internet to support alternative career paths. He lives in Antioch, California.

RICHARD NELSON BOLLES is the author of *What Color Is Your Parachute?*, the bestselling career-planning book in the world, which has sold more than ten million copies. It is updated annually. He has been a leader in the career field for more than thirty-five years. He lives in the San Francisco Bay Area.

## OTHER BOOKS BY

# Richard Nelson Bolles

**What Color Is Your Parachute? for Retirement**

*Planning Now for the Life You Want*

BY RICHARD N. BOLLES AND JOHN E. NELSON

6 x 9 inches, 288 pages

**What Color Is Your Parachute? for Teens**

*Discovering Yourself, Defining Your Future*

BY RICHARD NELSON BOLLES AND CAROL CHRISTEN

6 x 9 inches, 176 pages

50,000 copies sold!

AVAILABLE FROM YOUR LOCAL BOOKSTORE, OR ORDER DIRECT FROM THE PUBLISHER:

PO Box 7123, Berkeley, CA 94707

 29

www.tenspeed.com • order@tenspeed.com